M000166359

China's Belt and Road Initiative

~

Connecting Countries Saving Millions of Lives

ANDRE VLTCHEK

BADAK MERAH SEMESTA
2019

China's Belt and Road Initiative ~
Connecting Countries Saving Millions of Lives

Copyright © 2019 Andre Vltchek
All rights reserved

Proofreader: Arthur Tewungwa
Cover photo: Andre Vltchek
Cover design: Rossie Indira
Layout: Rossie Indira

1st edition, 2019

Published by PT. Badak Merah Semesta
http://badak-merah.weebly.com
email: badak.merah.press@gmail.com

ISBN: 978-602-50954-8-1

By the same author

Non-fiction:
"China and Ecological Civilization" (with John B. Cobb, Jr.)
"Revolutionary Optimism, Western Nihilism"
"The Great October Socialist Revolution: Impact on the World and the Birth of Internationalism"
"Exposing Lies of the Empire"
"Fighting Against Western Imperialism"
"On Western Terrorism: From Hiroshima to Drone Warfare" (with Noam Chomsky)
"The World Order and Revolution!" (with Christopher Black & Peter Koenig)
"Western Terror: From Potosi to Baghdad"
"Indonesia: Archipelago of Fear"
"Exile" (with Pramoedya Ananta Toer & Rossie Indira)
"Oceania – Neocolonialism, Nukes & Bones"

Fiction:
"Aurora"
"Point of No Return"
"Nalezeny"
"Plays: 'Ghosts of Valparaiso' and 'Conversations with James'"

Contents

Preface:
US – China "Trade" War?
No Way! Only the Defeat
of Turbo-Capitalism!

*I*t is very popular these days to talk and write about the "trade war" between the United States and China. But is there really one raging? Or is it, what we are witnessing, simply a clash of political and ideological systems: one being extremely successful and optimistic, the other depressing, full of dark cynicism and nihilism?

In the past, West used to produce almost everything. While colonizing the entire planet (one should just look at the map of the globe, between the two world wars), Europe and later the United States, Canada and Australia, kept plundering all the continents of natural resources, holding hundreds of millions of human beings in what could be easily described as 'forced labor', often bordering on slavery.

Under such conditions, it was very easy to be 'number one', to reign without competition, and to toss around huge amounts of cash, for the sole purpose of indoctrinating local and overseas 'subjects' on topics such as the 'glory' of capitalism, colonialism (open and hidden), and

Western-style 'democracy'.

It is essential to point out that in the recent past, the global Western dictatorship (and that included the 'economic structure) used to have absolutely no competition. Systems that were created to challenge it, were smashed with the most brutal, sadistic methods. One only needs to recall invasions from the West to the young Soviet Union, with the consequent genocide and famines. Or other genocides in Indochina, which was fighting its wars for independence, first against France, later against the United States.

***

Times changed. But Western tactics haven't.

There are now many new systems, in numerous corners of the world. These systems, some Communist, others socialist or even populist, are ready to defend their citizens, and to use the natural resources to feed the people, and to educate, house and cure them.

No matter how popular these systems are at home, the West finds ways to demonize them, using its well-established propaganda machinery. First, to smear them and then, if they resist, to directly liquidate them.

As before, during the colonial era, no competition has been permitted. Disobedience is punishable by death.

Naturally, the Western system has not been built on excellence, hard work and creativity, only. It was constructed on fear, oppression and brutal force. For centuries, it has clearly been a **monopoly**.

***

Only the toughest countries, like Russia, China, Iran,

North Korea or Cuba, have managed to survive, defending their own cultures, and advancing their philosophies.

To the West, China has proved to be an extremely tough adversary.

With its political, economic, and social system, it has managed to construct a forward-looking, optimistic and extraordinarily productive society. Its scientific research is now second to none. Its culture is thriving. Together with its closest ally, Russia, China excels in many essential fields.

That is precisely what irks, even horrifies the West.

For decades and centuries, Europe and the United States have not been ready to tolerate any major country, which would define its own set of rules and goals.

China refuses to accept the diktat from abroad. It now appears to be self-sufficient, ideologically, politically, economically and intellectually. And where it is not fully self-sufficient, it can rely on its friends and allies. Those allies are, increasingly, located outside the Western sphere.

***

Is China really competing with the West? Yes and no. And where "yes", it is often not done consciously.

It is a giant; still the most populous nation on earth. It is building, determinedly, its socialist motherland (applying "socialism with Chinese characteristics" model). It is trying to construct a global system which has roots in the thousands of years of its history (even BRI – Belt and Road Initiative, is often nicknamed the "New Silk Road").

Its highly talented and hardworking, as well as increasingly educated population, is producing, at a higher pace and often at higher quality than the countries in

Europe, or the United States. As it produces, it also, naturally, trades.

This is where the 'problem' arises. The West, particularly the United States, is not used to a country that creates things for the sake and benefit of its citizens. For centuries, Asian, African and Latin American people were ordered what and how to produce, where and for how much to sell the produce. Or else!

Of course, the West has never consulted anyone. It has been producing what it (and its corporations) desired. It was forcing countries all over the world, to buy its products. If they refused, they got invaded, or their fragile governments (often semi-colonies, anyway) overthrown.

In the eyes of the West, the most terrible thing that China is doing is: it is producing what is good for China, and for its citizens.

That is, unforgiveable!

***

In the process, China 'competes'. But fairly: it produces a lot, cheaply, and increasingly well. The same can be said about Russia.

These two countries are not competing maliciously. If they were to decide to, they could sink the US economy, or perhaps the economy of the entire West, within a week.

But they don't even think about it.

However, as said above, to just work hard, invent new and better products, advance scientific research, and use the gains to improve the lives of ordinary people (they will be no extreme poverty in China by the end of 2020) is seen as the arch-crime in London and Washington.

Why? Because the Chinese and Russian systems

appear to be much better, or at least, simply better, than those which are reigning in the West and its colonies. And because they are working for the people, not for corporations or for the colonial powers.

And the demagogues in the West – in its mass media outlets and academia – are horrified that perhaps, soon, the world will wake up and see the reality. Which is actually already happening: slowly but surely.

***

To portray China as an evil country, is essential for the hegemony of the West. There is nothing so terrifying to London and Washington as the combination of these words: "Socialism/Communism, Asian, success". The West invents new and newer 'opposition movements', it then supports them and finances them, just in order to then point fingers and bark: "China is fighting back, and it is violating human rights", when it defends itself and its citizens. This tactic is clear, right now, in both the northwest of the country, and in Hong Kong.

Not everything that China builds is excellent. Europe is still producing better cars, shoes and fragrances, and the United States, better airplanes. But the progress that China has registered during the last two decades, is remarkable. Were it to be football, it is China 2: West 1.

Most likely, unless there is real war, in ten years, China will catch up in many fields; catch up, and surpass the West. Side by side with Russia.

It could have been excellent news for the entire world. China is sharing its achievements, even with the poorest of the poor countries in Africa, or with Laos in Asia.

The only problem is, that the West feels that it has to

rule. It is unrepentant, observing the world from a clearly fundamentalist view. It cannot help it: it is absolutely, religiously convinced that it is obliged to give orders to every man and woman, in every corner of the globe.

It is a tick, fanaticism. Lately, anyone who travels to Europe or the United States will testify: what is taking place there is not good, even for the ordinary citizens. Western governments and corporations are now robbing even their own citizens. The standard of living is nose-diving.

China, with just a fraction of the wealth, is building a much more egalitarian society, although you would never guess so, if you exclusively relied on Western statistics.

***

So, "trade war" slogans are an attempt to convince the local and global public that "China is unfair", that it is "taking advantage" of the West. President Trump is "defending" the United States against the Chinese 'Commies'. But the more he "defends them", the poorer they get. Strange, isn't it?

While the Chinese people, Russian people, even Laotian people, are, 'miraculously', getting richer and richer, they are getting more and more optimistic.

For decades, the West used to preach 'free trade', and competition. That is, when it was in charge, or let's say, 'the only kid on the block'.

In the name of competition and free trade, dozens of governments got overthrown, and millions of people killed.

And now?

What is China suppose to do? Frankly, what?

Should it curb its production, or perhaps close scientific

labs? Should it consult the US President or perhaps British Prime Minister, before it makes any essential economic decision? Should it control the exchange rate of RMB, in accordance with the wishes of the economic tsars in Washington? That would be thoroughly ridiculous, considering that (socialist/Communist) China will soon become the biggest economy in the world, or maybe it already is.

There is all that abstract talk, but nothing concrete suggested. Or is it like that on purpose?

Could it be that the West does not want to improve relations with Beijing?

On September 7, 2019, AP reported:

> White House economic adviser Larry Kudlow compared trade talks with China to the U.S. standoff with Russia during the Cold War…
> *"The stakes are so high, we have to get it right, and if that takes a decade, so be it,"* he said.
> Kudlow emphasized that it took the United States decades to get the results it wanted with Russia. He noted that he worked in the Reagan administration: *"I remember President Reagan waging a similar fight against the Soviet Union."*

Precisely! The war against the Soviet Union was hardly a war for economic survival of the United States. It was an ideological battle, which the United States, unfortunately won, because it utilized both propaganda and economic terror (the arms race and other means).

Now, China is next on the list, and the White House is not even trying to hide it.

But China is savvy. It is beginning to understand the game. And it is ready, by all means, to defend the system which has pulled almost all its citizens out of misery, and which could, one day soon, do the same for the rest of the world.

10 September 2019

Belt and Road Forum in Beijing and How Western 'Reports' Are Smearing China

*T*he second Belt and Road Forum for International Cooperation took place from 25 th to 27th April, 2019. The Chinese President Xi Jinping delivered the keynote address.

It was an event of tremendous proportions and importance: leaders from 37 countries participated, including Russia's President Vladimir Putin and President Duterte of the Philippines. Beijing hosted 5,000 guests from 150 countries, as well as 90 international organizations.

The Belt and Road Initiative (BRI) has already been reshaping the world, fundamentally. Previously at the mercy of the Western imperialist powers, their armies, propaganda apparatuses and brutal financial institutions; Africa, the Middle East, Central and Southeast Asia have suddenly discovered that they have alternatives and choices. For various parts of the world, decades and centuries of stagnation and humiliation under colonialist and post-colonialist regimes have begun to come to an end. Entire nations have been freeing themselves, realizing their great hidden potential.

All this because of BRI; because of China as well as its close ally, Russia.

Entire huge railroad projects in East Africa as well as in the once devastated Laos (devastated by the insanely brutal Western carpet-bombing campaigns, which are still called a "Secret War") are now connecting continents. Along the railway lines, schools are growing, and so are medical facilities, community learning centers and cultural institutions.

But the BRI is not only about the economy, not only about infrastructure and development, it is above all about the well-being of the people, about the culture, health and knowledge. It is aiming at connecting human beings of different races, life philosophies, and beliefs.

And the rulers in the West are horrified. Nothing outrages them more than the prospect of losing absolute control over the world. For them, it is not (and never was) about improving the lives of hundreds of millions of impoverished individuals. They had centuries of absolute power over the planet, and all they did was to enrich themselves, murdering and robbing in all corners of the globe. For them, it is about 'winning or losing', about maintaining its colonies and 'client' states; by all means, even by the most brutal ones.

For China, (through BRI), it is all about spreading wealth everywhere. The firm belief in Beijing was and is: **If the world is doing well, China will prosper, too.**

And so, in Washington and London, and in so many other centers of Western might, thousands of 'professionals' are now employed and busy smearing China and its most ambitious international (and internationalist) projects. Smearing and spreading nihilism is an extremely well-paid job, and for as long as China is rising and the West declining, it appears to be a permanent one. There will be no deficit when it comes to funding all those anti-Chinese 'academic reports', fake analyses and articles. The more of them, the better; the more ridiculous they get, the better remunerated they are.

Take this one, for instance: "Grading China's Belt and Road" by the Center for a New American Security (CNAS).

With all those footnotes and 'references', it looks professional and academic. It can impress millions of China-phobes and China-bashers in Europe and North America. Suffering from complexes of superiority and "Yellow-Peril mentality", they are searching for, and then welcoming all vicious attacks against Beijing and its initiatives.

Look closer, and it is 'reports' like this that are clearly nothing more than thinly disguised propaganda work ordered by those who are aiming at discrediting China and its internationalist efforts.

In its Executive Summary, the report states:

Since its launch in 2013, what China calls "One Belt, One Road" has emerged as the corner- stone of Beijing's economic statecraft. Under the umbrella of the Belt and Road, Beijing seeks to promote a more connected world brought together by a web of Chinese-funded physical and digital infrastructure. The infrastructure needs in Asia and beyond are significant, but the Belt and Road is more than just an economic initiative; it is a central tool for advancing China's geo-political ambitions. Through the economic activities bundled under the Belt and Road, Beijing is pursuing a vision of the 21st century defined by great power spheres of influence, state-directed economic interactions, and creeping authoritarianism.

As Beijing prepares to host the second Belt and Road Forum in late April 2019, countries that once welcomed Chinese investment have become increasingly vocal about the downsides. This report is intended to serve as a resource for governments, corporations, journalists, and civil society groups now re-evaluating the costs and benefits of Belt and Road projects...

In brief, it is propaganda; anti-Chinese propaganda, anti-Communist (or call it 'anti-central-planning-propaganda).

It is also a tool for all those who are ready to criticize China, defining its marvelous efforts as a 'debt trap', among various other derogatory terms.

A leading academic at the University of the Philippines (U.P.), Roland G. Simbulan, agreed to analyze the origin of the CNAS report for this essay:

The April 2019 Report "Grading China's Belt and Road" by the Center for a New American Security (CNAS) seems to be one of the latest findings and studies of American conservative think tanks which are in fact aimed at discrediting China's economic thrusts through China-financed infrastructure, land and sea transport, investments, etc. These are China's answer to the U.S.' global military build-up and encirclement of its fast rising rival superpower. China is trying to avoid the mistakes of the Western powers including the U.S. and the former USSR by not engaging in a tit for tat arms race. Instead, it is answering back with its Belt Road Initiative as well as other economic and market initiatives aimed at reinforcing China's strengths while avoiding a direct attack on where the U.S. is strongest and has more advantage: the U.S. global military forces.

It is obvious from the backgrounds of the CNAS fellows who are authors of the report that they are all connected with the U.S. Department of Defense, the U.S. Department of State and the U.S. National Security Council. The American Enterprise Institute is a quasi-U.S. federal government think tank composed of recycled officials of the U.S. Department of Defense and U.S. Department of State. It is also obvious that they have consolidated the economic and political reports of all the U.S. intelligence community which are coordinated by the U.S. National Security Adviser.

And obviously, CNAS is not hiding where it stands, ideologically. It quotes such right-wing warriors as the French President, Emmanuel Macron, the International Monetary Fund Managing Director Christine Lagarde, the Minister of Energy in the defunct and discredited Ecuadorian government, Carlos Perez, and other unsavory figures.

Roland G. Simbulan continues:

While the CNAS Report may indeed have identified some of China's vulnerabilities in the management of its China-funded projects which can easily merit criticism, i.e., sovereignty eroding, non-transparent, unsustainable financial burdens, locally disengaged, geopolitically risky, environmentally unsustainable, and corruption-prone), let us remember that China's BRI was only launched in 2013. The U.S. and its Western Allies, including the multilateral institutions that they have created to assure U.S. neoliberal control of national economies since 1945 have engaged in practicing these "challenges" and dangers that it accuses China of initiating through BRI projects "for China's geopolitical ambitions.

These may be valid as in the case of the 10 case studies identified by the CNAS Report. But it is too soon to make conclusions in such a short time from 2013-2018. For these are also practices that have long been inflicted by the U.S. Empire and its allies since the end of World War 2 to assure economic, political and military hegemony. Unintentionally, the seven (7) challenges or dangers of China's BRI identified by the CNAS are really challenges that are continually being inflicted by the U.S. Empire and its Western allies on weaker and smaller countries. Precisely, many countries in Asia, Africa and Latin America are turning towards alternative international institutions such as ALBA in Latin America and BRI BECAUSE of the onslaught that they have long experienced with the PAX AMERICANA i.e. the U.S. and its allies.

Can the CNAS show that their sponsors and patrons are doing better, or can do better? The best way for the U.S. to counter the Belt Road Initiative (BRI) is to show AND prove that they can offer a better deal with developing countries in need of assistance for their infrastructure and development projects.

***

Mr. Sidqy LP Suyitno, an Indonesian high government official and former State Finance and Monetary Analysis Director of the Ministry of National Development Planning, is also puzzled by some of the wording in the report. When asked about the BRI project to build the bullet train from the Indonesian capital Jakarta to its city of Bandung, he contradicted the report:

Geopolitically Risky? It seems NOT to be. It seems more like making bilateral relations with Japan uncomfortable. The Japanese have been enjoying the benefits when it comes to relations with Indonesia, ever since Suharto's dictatorship: the automotive industry is more like an oligopoly for Japanese cars in Indonesia. And what do we get back? We still don't have our own car industry, our national car or our own national motorcycles production. Even though we have a very large "captive market"; in 2018, 1.1 million cars & 6.5 million motorcycles were sold in Indonesia.

Apparently, what he is referring to, is that while Japanese car industry flooded Indonesia with its cars and badly polluting scooters, there were no benefits to the state or to the people of Indonesia. I can go much further and point out that according to my investigation, Japanese car industry corrupted the government officials in most of the Southeast Asian countries, "convincing them" not to build public transportation, instead choking both cities and the countryside with outdated models of private motor vehicles, consequently bankrupting citizens in the process.

In brief: Japan has managed to ruin Southeast Asian cities, preventing them from developing public transportation. And now should it be trusted in such places like Indonesia to develop a high-speed rail system? Indonesia, Laos and Thailand do not think they should trust Japan too much. They trust China much more. And the same goes for the Philippines. Malaysian Prime Minister, Mahathir Mohamad, when re-elected last year, stopped several high-profile projects with China, but now, it seems, has been re-discovering an appetite for cooperation with Beijing.

But the report speaks (using unacademic language, suddenly) about how China *poached* the high speed train project from the Japanese.

Professor Mira Lubis, from Tanjungpura University in Pontianak, West Kalimantan, Indonesia, stated for this essay, her hope that BRI could improve life and environment on her devastated island:

> From what I know about BRI, I believe that its efforts would be mutually beneficial for both Indonesia and PRC. In Southeast Asia, the focus of BRI will be what could be described as the Maritime Silk Road. Indonesia is an archipelago with over 17,000 islands. Since 2014, our government is aiming at transforming Indonesia into what it

calls the 'Global Maritime Axis'. It means, developing ports and shipping lanes among other vital projects. This would be in synergy with BRI; BRI could strengthen Indonesia as a maritime power.

My island, Borneo, is ecologically damaged. I hope that it could directly benefit from the cooperation with China and its BRI. China is at the forefront of the struggle for ecological civilization, and I believe in its wisdom. I'm optimistic that BRI might help to bring sustainable development to Borneo.

***

The CNAS report is 'all over the place', selectively attacking BRI and China for its involvement in Africa, South and Southeast Asia, the Middle East and South Pacific (Oceania).

In his essay *"China's road to a win-win ahead of BRI forum"* published by the *Asia Times*, renowned Brazilian analyst Pepe Escobar wrote:

> Relentless reports that the New Silk Roads, or the Belt and Road Initiative (BRI), are a perfidious neo-imperial debt trap set up by Yellow Peril 2.0 are vastly exaggerated.
>
> Beijing clinched a proverbial showering of BRI deals with 17 Arab nations, including Egypt, Lebanon and Oman. Not by accident, the forum this year was called Build the Belt and Road, Share Development and Prosperity. Up to 2018, 21 Arab nations had signed BRI memoranda of understanding.
>
> These nations are not only BRI partners, but 12 of them also went for strategic partnerships with China...

Little wonder why!

Say China or BRI in Africa, just pronounce those names, and most of the people will show great enthusiasm. Every, even the Western surveys, clearly indicate that all over the continent, people harbor extremely positive feelings forwards China.

In Kenya (where I used to live), I repeatedly heard those who were working on countless Chinese projects, repeat:

> This is the first time we are treated by the foreigners like human beings.

People in Europe and North America love to adopt 'politically correct speech', but words somehow do not translate into deeds. Chinese workers may sometimes be rough, but they treat Africans like brothers and sisters. They also try to compensate them as if they would be their own.

But the CNAS report only criticizes China's involvement in Africa, while African voices are rarely allowed to penetrate the uniform and dogmatic Western mainstream media cliches.

An influential Ugandan analyst and opposition figure, Arthur Tewungwa, wrote for this essay:

> The basic assumption of Africans is that they are stupid and ignorant of history, politics, and the global financial arrangement of the world. The scaremongering of Chinese global domination does not really wash on a continent that is still under a sustained attack from the very forces that led us into slavery, colonialism and its manifestation, neo-colonialism. Using the Ugandan opposition's criticisms of the government's (a staunch ally of the US and its regional sheriff) misuse and theft of Chinese aid while ignoring the fact that the same has been going on for the last 30 years with IMF and World Bank funds which the opposition has been criticizing, confirms that assumption.

Ugandans don't view China as a dangerous hegemon; they are still too busy trying to extract themselves from the current relationship with hegemon that has had its boot on the country's neck for the last 300 years. The opposition criticism was aimed at the conduct of America's principal, not the misrepresented intentions of China. The IMF and World Bank have not covered themselves in glory in Africa and ignoring that fact just plays more into China's hands.

***

In the South Pacific (<u>Oceania</u>) where I also spent several years of my life (writing a book about the plight of Melanesia, Polynesia and Micronesia), CNAS dishonestly criticizes the BRI project in Vanuatu.

Let me be brutally frank here: The West has almost ruined the entire Oceania by its unbridled consumption, by neo-colonialist policies; from the Solomon Islands to the Marshall Islands. Global warming has caused the near disappearance of such wonderful countries like Kiribati, Marshall Island and Tuvalu.

What has the West done to save them? Nothing! Just dumping junk food on Samoa and Tonga, on the Federated States of Micronesia, or on the Marshall Islands (RMI).

China has patiently and full-heartedly been trying to help: by planting mangroves, building anti-tsunami walls, elevating government offices, schools and medical posts up on stilts. It has built stadiums in order to improve the health of the desperately obese local population (on some islands, around 90% of the population are suffering from diabetes).

And what has the West done, after observing the great success of China? It went to Taiwan, and as the former Minister of Foreign Affairs of the RMI, Tony de Brum explained to me, began 'encouraging Taipei' to bribe local governments, so they would recognize Taiwan as an independent country; something that even the West has not done. As a result, predictably, Beijing was forced to break diplomatic relations and to withdraw its help. The result: Taiwan has done nothing for Oceania. Only the ordinary people in South Pacific have become the victims.

Now South Pacific countries are increasingly deciding to work with China. They finally understood who is their real friend.

Those South Pacific countries that 'stayed with China' are doing incomparably better. Why don't we hear about all this, from the West-sponsored reports? Why do we only read dirt, as well as nihilist speculation? Why not facts? Why not the truth, that it is the West that is destroying the world, and has been for decades and centuries?

***

BRI is not perfect, yet, but on the global scale, it is the best that humanity has right now. And it has been improving, month after month.

Ugandans had 300 years of horrors of 'Western democracy' and 'freedom'. Latin Americans have been beaten into submission for over 500 years.

In Washington, London and Paris, they love to say: "we are all the same". Such 'logic' washes out their crimes. It means: "everyone is as greedy and brutal as we are". But no, we are not the same! Cultures are different, on all corners of the globe. Some countries are expansionist, aggressive and obsessed with self-righteousness as well as complexes of superiority. Some are not. China is not. It never was. It never will be. If attacked or antagonized, it defends itself; and if threatened in the future, it will defend itself again. But it does not build its wealth on plunder, and on the corpses of the others, as the West has been doing for long centuries.

BRI is the exact contrast to the Western colonialism and imperialism. I say it not because I am defending some theory on these pages, but because I have seen the Chinese 'New Silk Road' in action, in places where I have lived and worked: Asia, the Middle East, Oceania, Latin America and Africa. In places where almost no one dares or cares to go: except for those few tough and 'insane' individuals like myself, and for the Chinese internationalists! I know such places intimately. Places where local people are almost never given an opportunity to speak; they never appear on the pages of the Western mass media, or on television screens, or in reports such as the one published by CNAS.

Until recently, their voices and lives mattered nothing. Now they do. They matter a lot.

These people exist; these people are alive; they want to breath, to live and to dream. I swear they do. And for them, especially for them, now exists the BRI!

25 April 2019

China's BRI Could Save Destroyed Southeast Asia

$\mathcal{M}$ost of the people in the West or in North Asia usually never think about it, but Southeast Asia is one of the most depressed and depressing parts of the world.

It has been through genocides, wars and atrocious military regimes. Then, there are those monstrous income disparities. According to The Bangkok Post, in 2018:

> The 10% poorest Thais had 0% wealth. 50% of the poorest Thais (25 million people) had 1.7% of the country's wealth while 70% (35mn) controlled 5%." In the same year, 1% of the richest Thais controlled 66.9% of the country's fortune.

Indonesia is not doing much better. In fact, if it were to provide correct, unmassaged statistics, it would easily overtake Thailand as the most unequal country on earth. But Indonesia does not even declare the precise number of people, as I was informed by my colleagues, UN statisticians. It still claims that it has around 270 million inhabitants, while in reality, even ten years ago, there were more than 300 million people living on the archipelago.

Except in the Communist Vietnam, super-rich Singapore, and (still) relatively wealthy Malaysia, poor people matter very little. Or more precisely, they do not matter at all. They do not exist. And poor people form the great majority in this part of the world, although you would hardly read it from the pages of official government bulletins.

It is enough to see Jakarta, Manila or Bangkok from the air, to understand that the Southeast Asian megapolises are totally fragmented, so they can serve the elites. Skyscrapers, malls and enormous hotels are surrounded by miserable houses and slums. Terribly inadequate public transportation (corrupt governments have been regurgitating every year, for decades, great numbers of cars and polluting scooters wishfully called 'motorbikes', instead of providing decent massive public transit systems) has made Jakarta and periodically Bangkok, some of the most polluted and depressing cities in the world.

Crime is out of control. Thailand has, per capita, according to Interpol, a higher murder rate than the United States. In the Philippines, before President Duterte came to power, cities such as Davao and Manila were suffering from some of the most horrid crime statistics in Asia. Indonesia, again, has escaped scrutiny, simply because of the absolutely amazing ability to hide the truth – most of the crimes committed there, particularly sexual ones, are never reported, and if reported, not registered.

The modern history of this part of the world is perhaps the most brutal on the planet. Brutal, but hushed up. The education system in Indonesia, Malaysia and Thailand is geared not to educate the children and young people about the monstrous genocides committed on the territory of Southeast Asia.

To mention just a few 'occurrences', the West murdered several million people in Vietnam, Laos and

Cambodia, during the so-called 'Vietnam War' and 'Secret War'. It carpet-bombed poor Laos and Cambodia, while supporting the most atrocious feudal regimes all over 'Indochina'. It also displaced millions of peasants. As a result, multitudes died from hunger.

Indonesia perpetrated three genocides, killing millions. First, during the 1965-66 one, triggered by the U.S.A. and its allies, murdered 1 – 3 million intellectuals, artists, teachers, Communists and members of the Chinese minority. The second was the U.S.A, U.K. and Australia-backed occupation of East Timor, which took lives of 30%-40% of the islanders. The third genocide is the on-going, horrendous occupation and plunder of West Papua.

Burma, broke and divided by British colonialism, is yet another story. And so are the monstrous Malaysian massacres, which took place in 1969. And various massacres of the opposition as well as of immigrants, in Thailand. The Thai bombing of Vietnam and Laos, to impress handlers in Washington. And the U.S. massacres in the Philippines, as well as the brutal civil war there, in Mindanao.

The list goes on and on. It is a brutal horror show, the never-ending awfulness of Western neo-colonialism, as well as the sleazy servility of local rulers.

The results are omnipresent: the beaches of entire countries are devastated and privatized. Whole enormous islands like Borneo, Papua and Sumatra are finished, scarred and poisoned by local and multi-national corporations. It is smoke and filth, clogged rivers, collapsed cultures. Entire ancient civilizations are wiped-out, converted to 4th rate replicas of Disneyland. No mercy, no compassion, no future.

But it is all hushed up. Crimes are denied. Outraged, confused nations are called 'lands of smiles', or "friendly and tolerant archipelagos'.

It is insane, but tens of millions of foreign tourists descend on this ruined part of the world, annually. They see nothing. Some like it. They only nurture their complexes of superiority here. They do not want to understand anything. They choose to be blind. Cheap sex, shitty alcohol and beach food, as well as monumental sunburns. They continue the demolition work which has been triggered by their governments and corporations.

***

The mood is terrible. In Indonesia, foreigners and even locals get insulted in the middle of the day, just for being 'different'. Whites are. Chinese are. Indians are. Black people are, with terrible regularity and brutality.

In Thailand, foreigners get killed and raped, for almost no, or very little reason. Rapes are as regular as sunburns. The terrible occurrences are reported almost weekly by the local and foreign press. Sometimes. Sometimes they are not.

Poor people feel that their beaches, their cities, their forests, have been stolen from them. In Indonesia, on the Bali and Lombok islands, everything has actually really been looted from the locals.

Societies have crumpled. The plunder of the resources, of nature, of everything, was already taking place for years and decades, even centuries.

No one knows the way out of this nightmare. Most of Southeast Asia knows nothing else than this subjugation. And it is not even called a nightmare. In Southeast Asia, or in the West which controlled these societies for as long as one can remember, the horror is being glorified.

***

And yet, yet... On the same continent, not far away, an enormous country, governed by the Communist Party, and professing 'socialism with Chinese characteristics', has been building a totally new society, defining and implementing an 'ecological civilization', pulling hundreds of millions of citizens out of poverty, constructing a great scientific base, the fastest trains on earth, massive mass transit systems in each and every city, first rate schools and universities, and stunning concert halls, opera houses and museums.

And all this with only a fraction of the financial resources, calculated on a per capita basis, of those of the West.

China... A country with 6,000 years of history and culture, with about 1.4 billion inhabitants, and with an absolutely, diametrically opposite economic and social system from that which was force-fed, for decades, to the people of Southeast Asia by the West.

A country, which, by 2020, as promised by her President Xi Jinping, will have no one, be it in the cities or in the villages, living in extreme poverty.

China, a country which is growing in order to serve its people. A country which is using capitalist companies in order to fulfill Communist and socialist goals. A country with a centrally planned and greatly successful economy. Where all land belongs to the government, and the entire future – to the people.

Imagine this country, near the decaying colossus of the mainly miserable, oppressed Southeast Asia. Southeast Asia, with mostly failed systems which has forced hundreds of millions of human beings to live in filthy, destitute cities and in the feudal countryside.

Just compare sinking, clogged, holessly polluted

Jakarta to Beijing, Shanghai or Xi'an!

And now, China, with its culture based on communalism and internationalism, is extending its hand, and basically saying: "Let us grow together! Let us help our people, let's struggle side-by-side for a much better world. Let us save, liberate, empower your hundreds of millions of men, women and children; let us protect them from hunger, illnesses, functional illiteracy and the lack of a decent future!"

All this, despite the fact that in Indonesia, Malaysia, Philippines and elsewhere, Chinese people were often treated like animals, killed and raped in countless pogroms, and kept away from participating in governing these countries.

This extension of the hand is called "BRI" – "The Belt and Road Initiative."

And it is, most likely, the greatest global and internationalist initiative in the history of humankind.

It is the most optimistic, truly socialist, vision for our planet, based on sharing and the genuine commonwealth of nations.

An enormous belt of high-speed railroads, roads, super-fast communication corridors, ports and airports, but also schools and universities, high-quality hospitals for all, of film studios and publishing houses, theatres and museums.

As this essay goes to print, China just inaugurated amazing, 4.300 km long railroad, cutting across Africa, from Tanzania to Angola. This project alone will save dozens of millions of lives. I worked in Africa, for several years. I lived there, making films, criss-crossing the continent.I know.

I have worked in more than 160 countries on this planet. I have seen a lot. But I have never encountered any vision so confident, so positively revolutionary, and at the same time, so kind.

***

The West will fight. It will do everything in its power to prevent the BRI from succeeding.

It will not let Southeast Asia go without a struggle. As it is not letting Central Asia go.

Recently, I analyzed the so-called "Uighur Issue", in my detailed report compiled in Turkey, Syria, Afghanistan and Indonesia – *"March of Uighurs"* it is called. The West and its allies are radicalizing, arming and militarizing the Uighur ethnic minority, doing all they can to sabotage the BRI, by attempting to destroy its important center – Urumqi – in Northwest China. This may slow the projects aimed at inter-connecting China, entire Central Asia, Iran, and even Turkey and parts of Russia.

The same has been happening in Southeast Asia. The West has unleashed a tremendous propaganda force; it has employed countless NGO's, as well as thousands of local 'academics' and 'journalists', trying to smear all China's attempts to pull the region out from slumber and above all, from the toxic dependency on Western colonialist powers.

I have been monitoring this occurrence, in among other places, the Philippines, where the administration of President Duterte has moved the country much closer to Beijing, and away from Washington, improving greatly the lives of the great majority of the Filipino people. President Duterte enjoys the support of around 80% of his citizens, but is brutally attacked by Western media and NGO's. He calls China "the kindest nation on earth". This can never be forgiven in the West.

The same can be said about Laos, where China is basically revamping everything; pulling this poor and historically ruined country back to its feet, by building a high-speed rail system, modern energy sector, while constructing hospitals, schools, and even brand-new cities. And what did West do in Laos? It fought a 'Secret War' here, a side-kick of the Vietnam War, basically carpet-bombing with B-52s, a big part of the countryside, killing hundreds of thousands of people, just 'preventively', so they do not become Communists. Washington Canberra, London and Bangkok never even apologized for these crimes against humanity.

Now when China is rescuing its neighbor, a fellow Communist nation (Laos), the West is blabbing nonsense about the 'environment' and 'debt-trap'. Anyone who bothers to travel to the Plain of Jars or other ruined parts of Laos, will discover minefields left after the carpet-bombings. People are still dying there, and Western companies which produced these monstrous cluster bombs do not even share technical specifications with the de-mining agencies. Great concern about the environment! Here, U.S. bombs are still used as village fences.

A similar situation in Cambodia.

And several other nations in the region, including Burma.

***

Nobody is laughing out loud, at those Western NGOs and propaganda outlets that are spreading lies and recruiting local "experts", academics and journalists, mainly because the West and its servile local regimes have managed to sweep their crimes, genocides and economical plunder, under the carpet. London and Washington are controlling "historical narrative". They are trying to be sole owners of the truth.

The downfall, or call it the near collapse of Southeast Asia, is not being defined as a downfall. Far from it.

Nowhere has brainwashing been so intense and so successful, as in this part of the world. The great majority of local people are nowhere near to even beginning to comprehend what had been done to them. People do not know that they are the true victims, or that a different world is actually possible.

The Brits, Dutch, French, Portuguese and Spaniards, have all managed to get away with the looting and murder, mainly because 'education' has been shaped by the local 'elites', read: shameless treasonous servants of the Western imperialism. Talk to 'educated' (pro-British) Malaysians; read the books of their contemporary writers (almost all funded and dictated 'from abroad'). Then you will understand.

The United States is still admired in Indonesia, a country thoroughly impoverished and ruined by Washington's greed and geopolitical ambitions.

But Indonesia with a quality of life equal to that of poor Sub-Saharan African countries, is not officially considered to be poor, or deprived, or fascist or even feudal. Nobody seems to be questioning its ridiculously perverted statistics. The Philippines, too, was not defined as poor and destitute, before the arrival of President Duterte, even as millions were fleeing to all corners of the world, attempting to make living often under horrid conditions, in places such as the Gulf.

No one is laughing, because people were stripped off their ability to compare. The glorification of capitalism and imperialism has been too powerful. As has the smearing of

Communism.

And as has been the professional and consistent attempts to discredit everything Chinese, first by the racist European colonialists, and later by Cold War warriors and propaganda gurus from Washington and London.

***

China led by the Communist Party; socialist China with its own characteristics, is clearly misunderstood. Western propagandists are making sure that it is unappreciated. The BRI is also, and absolutely, misjudged. Not because it is not transparent – transparent it is. But because Western propaganda is, so to speak, constantly and professionally muddying the waters.

Everything about China's success is turned upside-down. The biggest fear, total horror, of the West and its lackeys in the new type of colonies here, is that China is both Communist, and a tremendously successful nation.

I am not going to argue here whether China is Communist or not, and if it is, to what extent. To me, it clearly is. Both Communist and successful. As well as internationalist. That is why I am decisively on its side, and on the side of Presiden's Xi Jinping's brainchild: BRI.

What is indisputable is that the intentions of the West to discredit both the PRC and BRI have absolutely nothing to do with trying to find solutions to the horrid problems our world in general, and Southeast Asia in particular, are facing.

The West does not want to find solutions. It wants Southeast Asia to remain ignorant, divided and servile.

The intentions of the West are clearly self-serving. Their only goal is to keep control over this resources-rich part of the world. And to prevent China from gaining its rightful position in Asia and the world.

For centuries, the West kept plundering, killing and enslaving Southeast Asian people. That simple. Full stop. The nightmare is continuing, to date. This time, local elites are fully involved, although, frankly, they were always involved, acting shamelessly as go-betweens for the colonialists and the enslaved people.

It is time to try a different approach. An approach which has already saved hundreds of millions of people from misery; by giving them new lives, education, health, culture and dignity. An approach which now puts ecology and the quality of life well above business and economic growth.

The people of Southeast Asia have to be informed about the choices they have.

It will not be easy, as there is no free, no alternative press there. The mass media and 'education' are controlled by the elites who, naturally, want to maintain the *status quo*.

But there are choices. For the first time in many years. Once the people of Southeast Asia know the truth, colonialism will end. Rapidly, almost immediately.

China and its system are showing great example by their deeds, not just by words. Wherever China comes, new winds are blowing. New societies are beginning to grow. Rationality blossoms. Nihilism disappears.

Soon a new chapter of Asian history will begin. The continent will be united, by belt and by road, by solidarity, determination and a great revolutionary spirit which will lead to the unstoppable renewal of this part of the world.

7 August 2019

Reason Why the West is Determined to Ignore China's Success

*I*t used to be comical, but suddenly it is not, anymore.

In the past, blind hatred towards China could had been attributed to ignorance, or at least to indoctrination by the Western propaganda, servile academia, and mass media outlets.

But now? China's tremendous leap forward, its excellent, humane social policies and determined people-oriented scientific research, as well as its march towards a so-called "ecological civilization" are well-documented, to the point that if anyone really wants to know, he or she has plenty of opportunities to learn the truth.

But it appears that very few want to learn. At least very few in the West.

China is seen negatively in almost all Western countries and their satellites. While surveys in places like Africa, where China intensively interacts with the people, helping them to break the chains of dependency on their neo-colonialist masters from Europe and North America, clearly indicate that it is admired and liked.

Last year (2018), a survey by the influential Pew Research Center ("Five Charts on Global Views of China") established that China is viewed mostly positively in non-Western countries: 67% in Kenya where China is involved in substantial infrastructural and social projects, 61% in the most populous African nation – Nigeria, 70% in the Arab country of Tunisia, 53% in the Philippines, despite the fact that there, the West has been fueling a dispute over the islands in the South China Sea, and 65% in Russia, which is now the closest Chinese ally.

In the U.K., 49% of citizens see China positively, 48% in Australia, but only 39% in Germany and 38% in the United States.

But what is truly shocking, is the attitude of the West towards the leadership of China's President – Xi Jinping – a determined thinker who is leading China towards true socialism with Chinese characteristics; almost eliminating extreme poverty (by the year 2020, there should be no pockets of misery left, anywhere on the territory of the PRC), and who is putting culture, a high quality of life, ecology and the general wellbeing of the Chinese people above economic indicators.

Conservative, anti-Communist Poland leads the pack: only 9% Poles "have confidence" in the leadership of President Xi. 11% of Greeks, 14% of Italians and 15% of Spaniards. That says something about Europe, as even in Canada, the number is 42%, and in the United States – 39%.

Is it truly just ignorance?

When interviewed by various Chinese media outlets, I am often asked the same question: "Why are we constantly criticized in the West, while we try to play by the rules, and doing our best to improve the planet?"

The answer is obvious: "Precisely for that reason."

***

Some 20 years ago, China and its socialist project, were still in the 'unfinished stage'. There were big differences in standards of living, between the urban areas in the east, and the countryside. Transportation was inadequate. Pollution in the industrial cities was very, very bad. Tens of millions of people were trying to migrate from the countryside to the cities, in search of jobs and a better living, putting great strains on the social system of the nation.

Those who did not like China, had plenty of 'ammunition', when criticizing it then. The country was moving forward, but the task to make it prosperous, clean, and healthy, appeared to by Sisyphean.

What followed was an absolute miracle, unprecedented in human history. Only the Soviet Union before the WWII registered greater growth and improvement of the standards of living of its people, than China did in the two last decades.

Everything in China changed. Its cities became clean, green, ecological, full of public parks, exercise machines for adults and children. Urban centers are now overflowing with a first class public transportation (all ecological), with impressive museums, concert halls, excellent universities and medical centers. Subsidized super-highspeed trains are connecting all major cities of the country. In Communist China, everything is planned by the government, top-notch experts, and by the Communist Party, and the private sector is there to serve the nation, not vice versa. It works. It works remarkably well. Citizens have much more say about how their country is governed, than those in the West.

Cities are clean, efficient, built for the people. No beggars and no slums. No misery. Things are getting better and better.

Foreigners who come to China for the first time are shocked: China looks much wealthier than the US or UK. Its streets, its airports, its metro systems, high-speed trains, theatres, sidewalks, parks, easily put those in New York or Paris to shame.

But, it is not rich. Far from it! China's GDP per capita is still relatively low, but that is precisely what makes "socialism with Chinese characteristics" so impressive and superior to the Western capitalism fueled by imperialism. China does not need to have average incomes of some $50,000+ per capita to prosper, to give its people an increasingly great life, to protect the environment, and to promote great culture.

Could it be, that this is precisely why the West, where everything is dependet on greed, is shaking in fear?

The West, where economic growth is everything, where people live in constant fear, instead of optimistic hope for the future. The West, where trillions of dollars and euros are wasted annually, so the elites can live in bizarre luxury and preside over irrational, unnecessary over-production and arms accumulation, bring no well-being to the majority.

China and its central planning are offering a much better and logical system, for its citizens and for the world.

Most of its science is geared to the improvement of life on this planet, not for cold profits.

President Xi's brainchild – BRI – is designed to lift up billions of people world-wide out of poverty, and to connect the world, instead of fragmenting it.

So why is President Xi so much disliked in Europe?

Could it be, that it is precisely because of the gigantic success of China?

***

Back to the previous point: 20 years ago, China had enormous social and environmental problems. The Westerners who did not like Communist Party of any type, would come and point fingers at things: "You see, Shanghai and Shenzhen are now prosperous, but look at other cities on the coast: see the contrast?"

Then the cities on the coast, all, began improving, planting parks, constructing universities, metros, beautiful streets.

Criticism from the West continued: "Now leave the coast, go west, and you will see how unequal China is!"

Eventually, the west of China improved so much, that there was virtually no difference between the quality of life in the cities there, and on the coast.

"It is all so cynical," the rant went on: "the difference between the cities and the countryside is so huge that peasants are forced to abandon their villages and seek jobs in the big cities."

Under the leadership of President Xi, the entire countryside received an enormous overhaul. Transportation, medical services, educational facilities and job availability improved so much, that in 2018, for the first time in modern history, people began migrating back from the cities to the countryside.

Now what? What next? "Human rights?" Not much to trash, anymore, if one sees with eyes open.

But the better China becomes, the more it cares about its people, as well as people all over the world, the harder it gets attacked.

Not one "Wow!" from Western regime and its mainstream media. Not one "China is now leader of the world in ecology, social policies, science, and virtually everything public."

Why?

The answer is obvious and unfortunately depressing: It is because the West does not want China and its president to succeed. Or if they succeed, it has to be hushed. The two systems are so different, that if China's one is correct, the Western one is wrong.

And the West is not searching for a concept that is good for the world. It only wants its own concept to survive and dominate the planet. Full stop.

That is why China is so popular in the countries which want to save their people from misery, and to build new, better societies. That is why China is smeared and disliked, even hated, in the West and in a handful of countries outside the West, where Westerners and their descendants are both ruling and controlling the mass media.

On a positive note, despite the determined and vicious propaganda being spread by Western and West-controlled mass media outlets, many more people have confidence in President Xi, than in the U.S. President Donald Trump, who inspires only 27% of the people all over the world.

17 July 2019

Panda Diplomacy Much Better than Mafia Extortion of Collapsing West

While the United States has been intimidating dozens of countries all over the world, two cuddly Chinese giant pandas – a three year old male called Ru Yi, and a female one year younger, named Ding Ding – were settling down in their new home, inside the legendary Moscow Zoo. Chewing bamboo shoots, and obviously enjoying the unprecedented attention, two specimens of iconic Chinese bears, were 'just there', in a good mood, making the entire world around them kinder and more secure.

As was reported by the RT:

Following the official talks at the Kremlin, Vladimir Putin and Xi Jinping went to the Moscow Zoo to meet the two giant pandas that have been handed to Russia by China as a "sign of respect and trust."

"When we talk about pandas, a smile appears on our faces," Putin told the journalists during a press-conference…

While the pandas are well taken care of, two great

countries – China and Russia – are now standing next to each other, united, and cooperating on countless fronts.

Both states and their leaders seem to come to many similar conclusions, identifying analogous goals: from scientific research that will bring benefits to our entire planet, to "ecological civilization" and the protection of the environment, from the energy sector, to the effective and wise extraction of commodities. From defense against the increasingly aggressive West, to meaningful cultural and educational programs and exchanges.

There seems to be no field in which the two nations could not compliment and cooperate with each other, finding great ways forward, for the benefit of their citizens and the world: communication technology, media, airplane industry, medical research, automotive industry, but also huge global projects like the Chinese BRI (Belt and Road Initiative) and Russian "Arctic road".

Both enormous countries – the most populous nation on Earth (China), and geographically the biggest one (Russia) – are constantly coming up with brilliant innovations that could improve, or even save, life on our planet – from organic farming to zero emission vehicles, ecological high-speed trains and new types of cities designed and built for a healthy, meaningful and cultural life of the citizens.

Some projects are 'profitable', but others are created simply in order to improve the quality of life, "Business is not everything", at least not in China and Russia.

Symbolically, the dollar is being ditched – China and Russia will be signing new contracts in their own currencies.

***

And what is the West doing?

Instead of building railroads, hospitals, schools and ecological farming, at home and in their present and former colonies, both North America and Europe are pushing entire countries against the wall: be they DPRK, Syria, Iran, Libya, Venezuela, Cuba or Nicaragua, to mention just a few.

Instead of joining great optimistic attempts to build a new and better world, the West is relentlessly smearing and antagonizing both Russia and China.

Every year, more and more money is allocated for propaganda against 'the enemies of the West'. Instead of creating and building, the West is spoiling all attempts to move our planet forward.

Entire religions as well as previously dormant ethnic conflicts are now being resurrected, funded and then used for one sole purpose: to destabilize two enthusiastic giants and their allies.

Yet, while ready to defend themselves if directly attacked, both Russia and China are using diplomacy, for as long as it is possible. The insanity of Western provocations is met with cool heads and admirable rationality.

At the same time, both Beijing and Moscow are increasingly determined to defend their allies, against direct attacks and 'regime change' lunacy. Syria, Venezuela and DPRK were high on the agenda, during the encounter of Presidents Xi Jinping and Vladimir Putin. It is clear that the good friends of China and Russia will not be allowed to fall.

***

Despite long centuries of looting, the West is in

irreversible decay. It is because its political, imperialist and economic system is obsolete, selfish and thoroughly depressing. It does not inspire people to work, to create, to sacrifice for the greater good, to invent and build a better planet.

Western rulers are aware of this. But they see nothing qwrong with *status quo*. Unwilling to change the regime, which serves the 'elites' in Europe and North America so well, they are spending huge resources on trying to 'deter' Russia, China and their allies. They are attempting to pervert the message from reaching all continents. They are also digging dirt, wherever they can find it, bombarding the world with every tiny unsavory detail about both Russia and China.

Entire armies of propagandists, psychologists, 'educators' and 'journalists' are being deployed, for the one and only goal: to smear, discredit and belittle the enthusiastic and positive efforts being made by Moscow and Beijing. Or in brief: in order to guarantee that our planet will continue to be plundered and exploited, with only a tiny minority benefiting.

The better the societies being built by China and Russia are, the louder the screams of those who are paid by the Western regime to uphold the repellant *status quo*.

***

Both Presidents Xi Jinping and Vladimir Putin are deeply concerned with the state of the world. It is obvious. Their governments are not being controlled by corporations – businesses have to obey the Communist Party of China, and the government of Russia.

"Democracy" is not when people can stick pieces of paper into big boxes, choosing between various political parties, if all of them are representing the same sclerotic system controlled by the elites and their lackeys. Democracy is the "rule of people", a system when countries are being built for the good of the citizens.

Chinese pandas are a powerful symbol; a promise of a kind and caring society. They are a symbol of a world built on emotions and decency, not on constant attempts to accumulate profit, to cheat, loot and murder.

Pandas are known to sit on their backsides, leisurely chewing bamboo shoots. They radiate a good mood, safety and kindheartedness.

And Pandas are what the Chinese government awards its friends with.

The presidents of China and Russia went together to the Opera House. And to the zoo. And they discussed the future; new roads, ecology and great future scientific achievements.

I like this kind of world. I like it very much. Don't you?

Enough of the bombing, and raping of entire nations and continents. Enough of "I will break your legs if you disobey".

I think most people on this planet want organic farming, an ecological civilization, exciting cities, fast trains, beautiful theatres and yes, gentle and good-natured bears.

12 June 2019

Now Indonesia in Love with Trains – China's BRI Ready to Help

$\mathcal{N}$ot long ago, they used to be an absolute disaster: Indonesian trains. Compared to the Dutch colonial era, the network has shrunk dramatically, from 6,811 km to 5,910km in 1950, and to a disastrous 3,000 km recently.

Just a few years ago, passengers used to climb onto the roofs of rusty dilapidated local carriages, often falling down to their death, or getting electrocuted. Often, trains were so terribly decrepit that the roofs would give way and people would fall down, also breaking floors in the process, finally ending up on the ground, in between the rails.

During the Suharto's pro-Western dictatorship, and also later, the train network was abandoned to its terrible fate; dirty, underfunded and primitive. The country and its corrupt officials concentrated on assembling and selling mostly Japanese cars and scooters, and on burning millions of gallons of gasoline. At some point, the situation became unbearable. By some counts, Indonesia has the most 'used' road system in the world: meaning, particularly in the cities, the traffic is so horrendous that it has begun to resemble 'total and permanent gridlock'.

Even corrupt officials had to recognize the fact that without a comprehensive railroad network, Indonesia simply couldn't survive.

President Joko Widodo began listening to his, and foreign advisers, who were pledging to improve, in fact to overhaul, the entire Indonesian rail network. But even before his administration, the real 'hero' of Indonesian railways emerged, Ignasius Jonan (born on 21 June 1963 in Singapore) who is now the Indonesian Minister for Energy and Mineral Resources. A former Indonesian Minister of Transportation, he headed the government-owned railway company, PT Kereta Api Indonesia (PT. KAI) from 2009 to 2014.

During his reign, the number of passengers increased by 50%, toilets at the stations and on board the trains became clean, and intercity trains began to run more or less on schedule.

The City of Jakarta purchased hundreds of second-hand but excellent Japanese suburban carriages, and dramatically increased the number of lines and frequency of the service, connecting the terribly overcrowded capital city with its suburbs, such as Tangerang, Bekasi and Depok, as well as with its neighboring city of Bogor.

Filthy, crumbling and dangerous stations received a total overhaul, now being equipped with escalators, elevators and relatively clean platforms.

The legend says that Mr. Jonan used to sleep inside the trains, often not having time to return home to rest. He achieved a lot, but much more has to be done.

After Mr. Jonan moved to another ministry, the work on the improvement of Indonesian rail services did not stop.

New intercity trains were added, and some innovative luxury services introduced, including carriages that resemble flat-beds in business class airplanes. But even the 'economy class' became comfortable and air-conditioned.

Hari Sungkari, an executive at BEKRAF (Indonesian Agency for Creative Economy) explained:

> Today PT KAI (Indonesian Railroad Company) has much better service than before. I am paying for comfort and punctuality, these days, things that are really important to me.

***

Tracks are the biggest problem. Most of them are outdated, single traction and non-electrified, as well as narrow; in brief – 1,067mm gauge.

Some are terribly old, often using viaducts spinning over the deep ravines, built a century ago. There are almost no railway tunnels in Indonesia, and even express inter-city trains have to habitually crawl when passing through the mountains, at sharp curves, hardly exceeding a speed of 10 kilometers per hour. That is true even about the most frequent passenger service between Jakarta and the third largest city in Indonesia – Bandung.

***

Java with nearly 200 million inhabitants and large, multi-million populated cities such as Jakarta, Surabaya, Bandung and Yogyakarta, has a similar shape as the Japanese island of Honshu (home to Tokyo, Osaka, Nagoya, Kyoto and other major cities), also over-populated, and also long and relatively narrow, while mountainous in the middle. In Japan, shinkansen bullet train lines have already managed to solve almost all intercity transportation troubles.

Much poorer Indonesia could never even dream about the introducing a bullet train network. Until now.

Losses from the city and inter-urban gridlocks became so horrendous, estimated in tens of billions of dollars annually that the Indonesian government had to start thinking 'big'. Huge investment into ports, airports, roads, and above all, rail, was desperately needed.

Studies were prepared. Japanese and Chinese companies began competing, for construction of the first stages of the inter-city high-speed train corridors.

Both the Japanese and Chinese systems are excellent, and have more strengths than weaknesses.

Japanese bullet trains are the oldest, the safest (no train has ever been derailed) and perhaps until now – the most comfortable, on earth.

China so far has managed to build the longest and the fastest high-speed rail network in the world, considering its length also amazingly safe and punctual.

There are certain serious problems with Japan in relation to Indonesia. For years and decades, Japanese companies producing cars and scooters, used Indonesia as an assembly line, regurgitating gas consuming and very outdated and stripped-down models of motor vehicles. Many say that Japanese car companies actually paid the Indonesian government officials *not* to build public transportation network in the cities.

Recently, I was told by Mr. Sidqy LP Suyitno, an Indonesian high government official and former State Finance and Monetary Analysis Director of the Ministry of National Development Planning:

> The Japanese have been enjoying the benefits when it comes to relations with Indonesia, ever since Suharto's dictatorship: the automotive industry is more like an oligopoly for Japanese cars in Indonesia. And what do we

get back? We still don't have our own car industry, our national car or our own national motorcycles production. Even though we have a very large "captive market"; in 2018, 1.1 million cars & 6.5 million motorcycles were sold in Indonesia.

He and many others in Indonesia have been actually supporting the Chinese bid.

And the Chinese bid finally won. Partially because the Chinese projects are cheaper than the Japanese, but also because the speed with which the Chinese are constructing new railroads, all over the world, cannot be matched.

The collapsed Indonesian infrastructure needs an extremely fast overhaul. And the Chinese firms can deliver, both high-speed railroad networks, as well as more modest (but equally important), express, cargo and local rail.

***

The tragedy of the Indonesian extreme capitalist 'economic' model is that the government does not have a large budget for infrastructure. It relies on foreign investment and on private companies. The Jakarta metro (until now, only one line) or the intercity lines are being constructed gradually, step by step; not simultaneously, all over the archipelago, which would be much more economic option.

The most logical first bullet train line project should be connecting two largest cities in Java, Jakarta and Surabaya, located approximately 1,000 km from each other. Such a line could move millions each day, as the shinkansen line between Tokyo and Osaka does. Such a mode of transportation would bring great relief to the overstretched and environmentally destructive road system.

But after countless 'studies' and debates, the Indonesian government has decided to first build the short stretch between Jakarta and Bandung, two cities only 138 km from each other by road (or 180 km by the slow, existing railway constructed by the Dutch more than a century ago). Today, the train journey takes 3h30mins and single traction does not allow more InterCitys to be deployed. Traffic jams on the highway often reduce driving to a crawl, or 20 km/h on average (6-7 hours in total).

China has already began building the bullet train line, and the estimated opening is at the end of year 2021.

Visiting the construction site near Bandung, I was told by a Chinese supervisor, that "everything is on target".

If all goes well, in approximately two years, the journey between Jakarta and Bandung should be reduced to 40 minutes.

The drawback is that both cities are choked by traffic jams and particularly in the case of Bandung, count with absolutely inadequate public transportation. Super-fast trains will be delivering passengers from one urban congestion nightmare to another.

Of course, China knows perfectly well how to resolve the problem, on both the intercity and urban level. That's what BRI is for. And Chinese cities are living testimonies of efficient and ecological urban planning.

But The Indonesian government has still no 'appetite' to go 'all the way'. It is still sticking to half-measures. Slow progress is leaving it behind even such countries like the Philippines, and Vietnam.

***

To give credit to Jokowi's administration in this field, it knows that without railroads, ports, airports and highways, there could be no progress in Indonesia. And his plans are truly 'Napoleonic'. When it comes to railways, he wants to build 12,000 km of tracks by the end of 2030, all over the archipelago. In Java, Madura and Bali alone, 6,900 km. Even 500 km in Papua. In Kalimantan (Borneo), 1,400 km, in Sumatra and Batam 2,900 km and in Sulawesi 500 km.

The new lines are supposed to be double traction, electrified and of wider gauge; not all, but at least some.

But here is the catch: China will either get deeply involved, and things will get constructed, or the entire dream will collapse, as so many Indonesian sand-castles have already vanished before.

Indonesia does not have the know-how nor stamina. China does.

Indonesia after the US-orchestrated coup in 1965, has been cannibalizing its natural resources, filling the pockets of a few rich and corrupt individuals, and building virtually nothing, regressing into one of the most under-developed nations in Asia.

Now BRI may change all this. Communist and highly enthusiastic, hardworking and internationalist China is raising the entire Africa from its knees. It can do the same for Indonesia, if the rulers in Jakarta allow it to do so. And if the Western propaganda and Western-paid NGO's do not succeed in derailing the entire national infrastructural revamp.

9 May 2019

City of Xi'an and Why the New Chinese Silk Road Terrifies the West?

Snow is falling on the wide sidewalks of the historic city of Xi'an, but people don't seem to be troubled by the bitter cold.

One of the oldest cities in China, Xi'an, is now vibrant, optimistic and stunningly beautiful. Sidewalks are paved with expensive stones and have more than enough space for pedestrians, electric bicycles, plants, trees and bus shelters.

Attempts by the Communist Party to turn China into an 'Ecological Civilization' are visible at every step: trees are revered and protected, comfortable walking is encouraged, while heavy duty, efficient and super modern public transportation is extremely cheap and ecological: the metro, and electric buses. All scooters are also electric, and so are the tricycles that are intended to transport passengers between the metro stations.

Compared to most Asian cities, but even to those in the United States and Europe, Chinese metropolises, including Xi'an, look like sort of urban areas of the future. But they are not 'impersonal', nor atomized. They are built for the people, not against them.

Xi'an is where the old Silk Road used to begin, connecting China to India, Central Asia and the Middle East.

It has a special significance and deep symbolism in Chinese history, and it is essential for China's present and future.

Xi'an is the oldest of the four ancient capitals, and home to the Terracotta Army of Emperor Qin Shi Huang. This tremendous world heritage site is a titanic symbol of loyalty, endurance and optimism. According to the legend, the entire tremendous army followed its commander to the other life, ready to defend him, to fight for him and if necessary, to offer the ultimate sacrifice. What does it all really mean? Is it just an emperor that these brave warriors are ready to sacrifice their lives for, with smiles on their faces? Or is it the nation, or perhaps even the entire humanity they are determined to defend?

Whatever it is, it is enormous, and seeing the sheer size of the monument sends shivers all over my body.

***

Some fifty kilometers away, at the North Station of Xi'an City, an army of the fastest trains on earth is lined up at countless platforms. These beautiful bullet trains connect Xi'an with Beijing, Shanghai and soon, Hong Kong. Some of them are already speeding towards the city of Zhangye, which is the first step on the new rail Silk Road that will soon continue all the way towards the north-western tip of China, at Kashgar. And Kashgar is only 100 kilometers from the border with Kyrgyzstan, and 150 kilometers from Tajikistan.

If someone thinks that China is simply a north Asian country, far away from the rest of the world, they should think twice. In the center of Xi'an, there is a bustling neighborhood, similar to those found in any energetic cities of the Middle East. There is a Grand Mosque, a bazaar, and endless lanes of colorful stalls, jewelry workshops, restaurants and *halal* eateries. Many women here wear colorful clothes and headscarves, while men cover their heads with skullcaps.

The western part of China is a vibrant mix of cultures from the north, as well as Central Asia. And the ancient capital of China – Xi'an – is well known and admired for its multi-cultural identity. Like the former Soviet Union, Communist China is an enormous and diverse country.

***

And the West doesn't like what it sees.

It hates those super high-speed trains, which, at tremendous speed, as well as cheaply and comfortably, cover distances of thousands of kilometers. It hates where they are going: towards the former Soviet Central Asian republics, and soon, hopefully, towards Afghanistan, Pakistan, Iran, Russia, and one day, maybe even India.

It hates the optimistic spirit of the people of Xi'an, as well as the wise and at the same time, avant-garde environmental policies of China.

It hates that in cities like Xi'an, there are no slums, no homeless people, and almost no beggars: that instead of advertisements, there are beautiful paintings with messages highlighting socialist virtues, including equality, patriotism, respect for each other, democracy and freedom. It hates that most of the people here look determined, healthy, in good spirits, and optimistic.

The West passionately hates the fact that China is essentially Communist, with a centrally planned economy and tremendously successful social policies (by 2020, China will eliminate the last pockets of extreme poverty), while striving for the ecological civilization.

China defies Western propaganda, which hammers into the brains of the people that any socialist society has to be drab, uniform and infinitely boring. Compared to such a city as Xi'an, even the European capitals look dull, depressing, dirty and in decline.

Yet China is not rich, not yet. At least on paper, (read: using statistics produced and controlled predominantly by the countries and by the organizations controlled by Washington, London and Paris), its HDI (Human Development Index, compiled by UNDP), is the same as Thailand's. While the contrast between two countries is striking. Thailand, a feudal society glorified by the West, because of its staunch support during the Vietnam War and because of its anti-Communist drive, is suffering from collapsed infrastructure (no public transportation outside Bangkok, awful airports and train system), monstrous, almost 'Indonesian-style' city planning (or lack of it), urban slums, endless traffic jams and basically no control of the government over business. Thailand has the most unequal wealth distribution on earth. In Thailand, frustration is everywhere, and the murder rate is consequently even higher than in the United States (per capita, according to INTERPOL data), while in China it is one of the lowest on the planet.

But above all, the West hates China's growing influence on the world, particularly among the countries that have been for centuries brutalized and plundered by European and North American corporations and governments. And it is scared that they will, eventually, fully understand that China is determined to stop all forms of imperialism, and to eradicate poverty in all corners of the world.

***

Xi'an is where the old and new Silk Roads have their starting points. The new one is called the Belt Road Initiative (BRI), and very soon it will account for tens of thousands of kilometers of railroads and roads connecting and crisscrossing Asia, Africa and Europe, pulling out of misery billions of men, women and children. Once completed, everybody will benefit.

There will also be countless new cultural institutions, film studios, concert halls, hospitals, scholls, community learning centers, 5G internet networks and many otrher innovations.

That is not how the West likes it. 'Everyone benefiting' is a totally foreign, even hostile concept, at least in the Western capitals. Only the West, plus those few 'chosen' and highly obedient countries (including Japan, South Korea and Singapore) have been, until now, allowed to prosper, forming a strictly 'by appointment only' club of nations.

China wants everyone to be rich, or at least not poor.

Most Asians love the idea. Africans love it even more. The new elegant train station in Nairobi, Kenya, is a new symbol, a promise of a better future. Tram lines in Addis Ababa, the construction of a high-speed train line that will go through Laos, all these are marvels unimaginable only a few years ago.

The world is changing, mainly thanks to the determined efforts of China and Russia to finally destroy Western colonialism (the 'project' that began so well right after WWII, but, except on paper, was never fully completed).

***

In our book "China and Ecological Civilization", a dialogue between leading philosopher John B. Cobb, Jr. and me, John who has been working very closely with the Chinese government on issues of environment and education, explained:

> As I compare China's success in giving serious attention to the well-being of its natural environment and needy citizens with that of European countries, my reason for betting on China is that I have some confidence that it will maintain governmental control of finance and of corporations generally. If it does this, it can also control the media. Thus, it has a chance of making financial and industrial corporations serve the national good as perceived by people not in their service. Less centralized governments are less able to control the financial and other corporations whose short-term interests may conflict with the common good.

That may be the main reason why the West is horrified, and trying to antagonize China by all means: If China succeeds, colonialism will collapse, but also corporatism, which, like a fairy-tale monster devours everything in its sight.

***

Facing thousands of determined Terracotta soldiers, I felt the enormity of China.

I imagined hundreds of millions of men and women building the nation; millions of construction sites, not only in China itself, but also abroad. I recalled my neighbors in Nairobi, when I used to live in Africa – optimistic, well-natured but tough Chinese engineers, who used to power-walk, together, every night. I liked, I admired their spirit.

To me, they were like present-day Terracotta soldiers: brave, determined and loyal. Loyal not to the emperor, but to humanity. Not military men, but people who are constructing, building a much better world in all corners of the globe, often with their own hands. Despite the vitriolic spite and nihilism unleased against them by the West.

In Xi'an, I stood in front of the old gate, where everything began, many centuries ago; the old Silk Road. Now, everything was returning here, in a grand circle. The new beginning.

It was cold. It was beginning to snow. But I was immensely happy to be here, and I felt alive and full of optimism for the future of humanity.

I made a few symbolic steps. Millions did before me. Millions will, again, soon.

20 February 2019

China Creates, Macau Burns and Robs

*I*t is truly an amazing site: monstrous US hotels and casinos, just few hundred meters from the Mainland China. All that kitsch that one usually associates with Las Vegas or Atlantic City, but bigger, much bigger! In fact, Macau is the biggest casino sprawl in the world.

Casinos, most of them confined inside the US-owned mega-hotels, make approximately 5 times more money here, than in Las Vegas.

You want Venetian; a tremendous mind-blowing temple of bad taste, complete with a fake San Marco Square, canals, gondolas (gondoliers don't sing O Sole Mio, thank God, as they are mostly from Portugal) and overcooked pasta – it is all here; one of the largest buildings on earth, and the biggest casino in the universe!

You want Parisian; yet another vulgar monstrosity, complete with a fake Eiffel Tower which lightens up right after dark to the great delight of the armies of selfie-takers? It is also here, in Cotai, Macau, together with the fake Champ de Mars that doubles as an (phony again) ice-skating rink.

Macau is tiny, measuring only some 115 km square. But with around 650,000 people, it is one of the most over-populated places in the world. There is no space to move around here, anymore. Macau is a total, thorough urban nightmare and failure, propelled and 'justified' only by greed. But its plans are still Napoleonic. The territory wants more and more. Or more precisely: the Macau government, together with big business from the West, want more and more visitors, more and more casinos, luxury retail stores, and of course, profits.

24 hours a day, 365 days a week, Macau sucks in like a monstrous turbine, millions, in fact billions of dollars, yuan or whatever currency manages to enter its territory. It attracts like a magnet, masses of people from the PRC, who are often still naïve, innocent and defenseless when confronted by brutal and extreme forms of capitalism and its advertisements.

In January 2019, I visited several casinos in Macau, and not surprisingly, there are very few traditional roulette tables there, but masses of electronically controlled machines. Everything is noisy, confusing and lacking transparency. Western casinos treat Chinese people like some brainless children. At least the classic roulette mainly wins (for casino) on 'neutral' 0 (zero), giving a gambler very fair chance. But electronic, futuristic machines are a sham, and can 'strip' an unseasoned gambler of everything, in just a few hours, even minutes. But that is, obviously, precisely the goal.

I am horrified to see hordes of good Chinese (PRC) citizens who work hard, building their beautiful country, and then crossing to that fake universe of Macau, where they are literally blowing their savings in spasmodic, insane sprees.

On 23 January, 2019, CNN reported from Hong Kong:

> Chinese authorities say they have busted an underground money-smuggling ring used to launder more than $4.4

billion through the Asian gambling hub of Macau.

The case is a high-profile example of Beijing's crackdown on attempts to dodge its capital controls, which it has tightened in recent years to prevent money from flooding out of the country and destabilizing the economy.

Macau's Judicial Police said the syndicate was formed in 2016 and relied on point-of-sale machines — the devices used by shops to conduct transactions with credit cards or debit cards — which were smuggled in from China.

These in theory would allow Chinese citizens to make withdrawals from their bank accounts that appeared to be domestic transactions, thereby avoiding China's strict limits on how much money people can move across its borders.

In theory, Chinese citizens are only allowed to take out of country no more than 100,000 Yuan, which amounts to approximately $15,000 annually. But local businessmen and gangs are always looking for loopholes.

Macau gangs are brutal and they are dealing with huge amounts of money. Antagonizing them is dangerous. Even journalists and academics connected to this tiny but super rich territory, prefer not to speak openly; only on condition of anonymity. One of my good colleagues replied, sarcastically, to my request for a quote:

I don't think I could contribute anything to your open eyes approach – and for me to write the truth on what I see in this fishing village making firecrackers turned capitalist paradise of Macau would be like you risking lèse-majesté in Bangkok by mocking the golden towers of the royal palace.

***

In the old, Portuguese historic area of Macau, which happens to be a UNESCO-inscribed world heritage site, there is hardly any place left to move. Weekends are the 'deadliest', with monstrous 'pedestrian traffic jams' and more than one hour-long taxi lines. However, weekdays are not much better.

Beijing tried to crack down on gambling and for some time it worked, but during the last months, casinos have been bouncing back. The loopholes are too numerous. In the meantime, the territory panicked ('God forbid it could not make as much money as before!') and began trying to attract even more tourists, mainly from the Mainland, by all means available: a new bridge, advertisements... It also began to cater to the lowest of tastes; historic houses have been painted in kitschy pink, vulgar bluish and greenish, as well as yellow colors. Culture and art has almost disappeared. And everything has become mass-produced and fake, including 'Portuguese food'.

Frankly, all that Macau represents is wrong: it has already ruined millions of human lives through mass gambling. It robs Mainland China of billions of dollars. Instead of educating people, it offers fake culture, in fact a disgusting parody on great cultural treasures of the world, 'Las Vegas-style'. It is brainwashing Chinese people, so they see the world through the eyes of Disney, Hollywood and big US hotel chains.

Many hotel managers come from Portugal (for 'authenticity' purpose, I suppose). They are arrogant, more North American than North Americans themselves, ambitious and unscrupulous. Many of them speak about Mainland China sarcastically, with spite. Typical Western 'democracy' and 'freedom of speech' nonsense.

And so, stripped of authenticity and decency, Macau adopted a gold-digging, repulsive 'culture'. Talk about 'fake news' and fake culture! Everything that is fake, is here, in Macau.

Across the water, in the PRC, beautiful modern cities

are growing, simple, elegant, and confident; built for the people.

In Macau, morale, socialist spirit, as well as family savings, are getting ruined and burned.

'One country two systems' has gone too far in Macau. This territory produces nothing. Not even those traditional firecrackers, perhaps. It only consumes, and perverts.

One of Sheraton Macau's employees, a Philippine lady born in Macau, explained:

> I don't recognize my own home city, anymore! It used to be a dormant, beautiful place. Now it is thoroughly ruined.

I don't recognize Macau either. And people who come here, from Mainland China, tend to change, quickly. Is this yet another Western subversion, an attempt to break China into pieces? Definitely. The government of the PRC should take more decisive action, soon; protecting its people and funds.

2 February 2019

Andre Vltchek

Why is Japan so Bitter About Unstoppable Rise of China?

*T*here used to be a pair of beautiful swings for children, not far from an old rural temple in Mie Prefecture, where I used to frequently powerwalk, when searching for inspiration for my novels. Two years ago, I noticed that the swings had gotten rusty, abandoned, and unkempt. Yesterday, I spotted a yellow ribbon, encircling and therefore closing the structure down. It appears that the decision had already been made to get rid of the playground, irreversibly.

One day earlier, I observed an old homeless man sleeping right under a big sign which was advertising a cluster of luxury eateries at the lavish Nagoya train station.

And in the city of Yokkaichi, which counts some 350,000 inhabitants, almost all but very few bus lines had disappeared. What had also disappeared was an elegant and unique, shining zodiac, which used to be engraved into the marble promenade right in front of the Kintetsu Line train station, the very center of the city. The fast ferry across the bay, connecting Yokkaichi with Centrair International Airport that serves Nagoya and in fact almost the entire area of Central Japan, stopped operating, as the municipal subsidies dried up. Now people have to drive some seventy kilometers, all around the bay, burning fuel and paying exuberant highway tolls and airport parking fees, to make it to their flight. What used to constitute public spaces, or even just rice fields, is rapidly being converted into depressing parking lots. It is happening in Central Japan, but also as far southwest as the city of Nagasaki, and as north as Nemuro.

Homeless people are everywhere. Cars (Japan now has more cars per capita than the United States) are rotting in the middle of rice fields and at the edges of once pristine forests, as they lose value rapidly, and it costs a lot of money to get rid of them properly. Entire rural villages are being depopulated, in fact turning into ghost towns. There is rust, bad planning and an acute lack of anything public, all over the country.

Japan is in decay. For many years, it was possible, with half-closed eyes, to ignore it, as the country was due to inertia hanging on to the top spot of the richest nations on Earth. But not anymore: the deterioration is now just too visible. Same as in the West.

The decay is not as drastic as one can observe in some parts of France, the United States, or the UK. But decay it is. The optimistic, heady days of nation-building are over. The automobile industry and other corporations are literally cannibalizing the country, dictating its lifestyle. In smaller cities, motorists do not yield on pedestrian crossings anymore. Cars are prioritized by urban planners, and some urban planners are paid, bribed by the car industry. Many areas can now only be reached by cars. There are hardly any public exercise machines, and almost no new parks. Japan, which prides itself on producing some of the most refined food, is now fully overwhelmed by several chains of convenience stores, which are offering unhealthy foodstuff.

For generations, people were sacrificing their lives in order to build a prosperous, mighty and socially balanced Japan. Now, there is no doubt that the citizens are there mainly to support powerful corporations or in short: big business. Japanese used to have their own and distinct model, but now the lifestyle is not too different from one that could be observed in North America or Europe. For the second time in its history, Japan has been forced to 'open to the world' (read: to Western interests and to the global capitalist economy), and to accept the concepts that used to be thoroughly alien to the Asian culture. The consequences were quick to arrive, and in essence, they have been thoroughly disastrous.

***

After WWII, Japan had to accept occupation. The Constitution was written by the US. Defeated but determined to rebuild and join the ranks of the richest countries on earth, Japan began collaborating with the West, first supporting the brutal invasion to Korea (the so-called "Korean War"). It totally gave up on its independence, fully surrendering its foreign policy, which gradually became indistinct from that of the United States in particular, and the West in general. The mass media has been, since the end of the war to now, controlled and censored by the regime in Tokyo. Major Japanese newspapers, as well as the Japanese national broadcaster NHK, would never dare to broadcast or publish any important international news, unless at least one major US or British mainstream media outlet had set the tone and example of how the story should be covered by the mass media in the 'client' states. In this respect, the Japanese media is not different from its counterparts in countries such as Indonesia or Kenya. Japan is also definitely not a 'democracy', if 'democracy' simply means the rule of the people. Traditionally, Japanese people used to live mainly in order to serve the nation, which was perhaps not such a bad concept. It used to work, at least for the majority. However, now, they are expected to sacrifice their lives solely for the profits of corporations.

People in Japan do not rebel, even when they are robbed by their rulers. They are shockingly submissive.

Japan is not only in decay. It tries to spread its failure like an epidemy. It is actually spreading, and glorifying its submissive, subservient foreign and domestic policies. Through scholarships, it is continuously indoctrinating, and effectively intellectually castrating tens of thousands of willing students from the poor Southeast Asian nations, and other parts of the world.

***

In the meantime, China, which is literally 'next door', is leading in scientific research, in urban planning, and in social policies. With 'Ecological Civilization' now part of its Constitution, it is way ahead of Japan in developing alternative sources of energy, public transportation, as well as organic food production. By 2020, there will be no more pockets of extreme poverty on the entire huge territory of China.

And in China, it is all done under the red Communist banners, which the Japanese public has been taught to despise and reject.

Tremendous Chinese determination, zeal, genius and socialist spirit are evidently superior, compared to the sclerotic, conservative and revanchist spirit of modern

Japan and of its handlers in the West.The contrast is truly shocking and very clearly detectable even with unarmed eyes.

And on the international stage: while Japanese corporations are plundering entire countries, and corrupting governments, China is helping to put entire continents back on their feet, using good old Communist internationalist ideals. The West does its best to smear China and its great efforts, and Japan is doing the same, even inventing new insults, but the truth is more and more difficult to hide. One speaks to Africans, and he or she finds out quickly what goes on. One travels to China, and everything becomes even clearer. Unless one is paid very well not to see.

***

Instead of learning and deciding to totally change its economic and social system, Japan is turning into a sore loser. It hates China for succeeding under its independent policies, and under its Communist placards. It hates China for building new and beautiful cities designed for the people. It hates China even for doing its best to save the environment, as well as the countryside. And it hates China for being fully independent, politically and socially, even academically.

China tried 'playing' footsies with the Western academia, but the game almost turned deadly, leading to ideological infiltration and the near collapse of China's intellectual independence. But at least the danger was identified, and the Western subversion was quickly stopped, just 5 minutes to Midnight so to speak; before it was too late.

In Japan, submission and collaboration with the

Western global imperialist regime is worn as some code of honor. Japanese graduates of various US and UK universities frame their university diplomas and hang them on the wall, as if they'd symbolize great proof of their success, instead of collaboration with the system which is ruining almost entire planet.

***

I remember, some fifteen years ago, Chinese tourists would stand on the bullet train platforms all over Japan, with their cameras ready, dreaming. When train would pass, they'd sigh.

Now, China has the most extensive and the fastest bullet train network in the world. Their trains are also more comfortable and incomparably cheaper than the Japanese or French ones; priced so everyone can afford to travel.

Chinese women used to eye, sadly, the offerings of Japanese department stores. iPhones were what the middle class was dreaming of possessing. Now Chinese visitors to Japan are dressed as elegantly as the locals, iPhones are not considered a luxury, and actually, Huawei and other Chinese manufacturers are now producing better phones than Apple.

I also remember how impressed Chinese tourists to Japan were with the modern architecture, international concert halls, and elegant cafes and boutiques.

Now, the cultural life of Beijing and Shanghai is incomparably richer than that of Tokyo or Osaka. Modern architecture in China is much more impressive, and there are innovations in both the urban and rural life of China, that are still far from being implemented in Japan.

While public playgrounds in Japan are being abandoned or converted into parking lots, China is building new parks, huge and small, recovering river and lake areas, turning them into public spaces.

Instead of omnipresent Japanese advertisements, China is placing witty and educative cartoons speaking about socialist virtues, solidarity, compassion and equality, at many arteries, even at the metro trains. Ecological civilization is 'advertised' basically everywhere.

Japanese people are increasingly gloomy, but in China, confident smiles are seen at each and every step.

China is rising. It is unstoppable. Not because its economic growth (government is actually not interested in it, too much, anymore), but because the quality of life of the Chinese citizens is going steadily up.

And that is all that really matters, isn't it? We can clearly improve the life of people under a tolerant, modern Communist system. As long as people smile, as long they are educated, healthy and happy, we are clearly winning!

***

Some individuals are still chasing those magic images of pristine Japanese forests and lakes. Yes, they are still there, if you search very hard. Tea rooms and trees, lovely creeks. But you have to work very hard, you have to edit and search for the perfect angles, as Japanese cities and countryside are dotted with rotten cars and weird metal beams, concrete wave breakers, with unkempt public spaces, with ugly electric wires hanging everywhere. As long as money can be saved, as long as there is profit, anything goes.

Japanese people find it hard to formulate their feelings on the subject. But in summary: they feel frustrated that the country they used to occupy and torture, is doing much better than their own. To Japanese imperialists, the

Chinese were simply 'sub-humans'. It is never pronounced, but Japan has only been respecting Western culture and Western power. And now, the Chinese 'sub-humans' are exploring the bottoms of the oceans as well as the space, building airplanes, running the fastest trains on earth, and making wonderful art films. And they are set on liberating the oppressed world, through its 'Belt and Road Initiative', and through other incredible ideas.

And what is Japan doing? Selfies and video games, idiotic meaningless nihilist cartoons, brainless social media, an enormous avalanche of uninventive pornography, of decorative 'arts', pop music and mass-produced cars. Its people are depressed. I have three decades of history with Japan, I know it intimately, still love it; love many things about it, but I also clearly see that it is changing, in fact collapsing. And it is refusing to admit it, and to change.

I work with China, because I love where it is going. I like its modern Communist model (I was never a great supporter of the "Gang of Four" and their cult and glorification of poverty) – let all Chinese people be rich soon, and let the entire oppressed world be wealthy as well!

But that is not what Japan wants. For some time, it felt 'unique'. It was the only rich Asian country. The only Asian country allowed to be rich, by the West. During apartheid, in South Africa, the Japanese people were defined as "honorary whites". It is because they had embraced Western culture. Because they opted to plunder the world, together with the Europeans and North Americans, instead of helping the subjugated nations. In many ways, it was a form of political and moral prostitution, but it paid well; extremely well, so its morality was simply not discussed.

Now China is getting ahead simply because of its

courage, hard work, the genius of its people, and all this, under the wise leadership of the Communist Party and its central planning. Precisely under things that the Japanese people were brainwashed into hating.

This is frustrating. It is scary. So, all that submission, humiliation and bowing to the empire was for nothing? In the end, it is China, it is Communism which will win, and which will be doing the greatest service to humanity.

Yes, Japan is frustrated. These days, polls speak of some 80% of the Japanese disliking the Chinese.

As I interact with people from all corners of Japan, I am getting convinced that the Japanese public subconsciously feels that, for decades, it has been betting on the 'wrong horse'. It is too proud to verbalize it. It is too scared to fully reflect on it. But life in Japan, at least for many, is clearly becoming meaningless, gloomy and depressing. And there is no revolution on the horizon, as the country was successfully de-politicized.

China is building, inventing, struggling and marching forward, confidently, surrounded by friends, but independently.

Japan is tied up and restrained. It cannot move. It doesn't even know how to move, how to resist, anymore.

And that is why Japan hates China!

11 January 2019

Laos – China is Building, West is Destroying and Spreading Nihilism

*I*t is one of those complex stories that are so difficult to tell, and yet they should, they have to be shared.

Imagine the splendid Mekong River, as it flows not far from an ancient capital of Laos, Luang Prabang. The river is powerful, with muddy banks, surrounded by lush mountains. Imagine poor villages and old ferry crossings, as well as broken plastic sandals on the feet of local people.

Then suddenly, near the village of Phonesai, you can spot several tremendous concrete pillars. They are growing out from the water, and from both river banks, literally connecting two mountains.

Soon it will be a bridge for high-speed trains. It is being built by China, a nation with the most advanced high-speed rail technology on earth. And a bit below, there will be another bridge, for cars and pedestrians.

Both mountains are being drilled, carefully and sparingly. This is where two tunnels will be passing through.

It is of course much cheaper to blow the mountains down with explosives. But earlier this year, China engraved the "Ecological Civilization" into its Constitution, and what it preaches at home, it also implements abroad.

This is the biggest project in the history of Laos, and it is often described as a mammoth engineering task: with 154 bridges and 76 tunnels, as well as 31 train stations. The Laotian terrain is very complex, its nature still pristine at large, and it is supposed to remain as such. The railroad will be 414 kilometers long, connecting Boten on the Laos-China border and the Laotian capital Vientiane. It is estimated that 20,000 Chinese workers will take part in the construction, as well as further tens of thousands of local laborers.

The railroad is expected to be operational in 2021, linking Laos with both China in the north, and Thailand to the south.

China Daily reported:

> The Lao government hopes that the completion of China-Laos railway will bring powerful momentum to social and economic development, while the construction of the railway has already brought great changes in many areas along the route.
>
> At Sinohydro Bureau 3 Co Ltd's railway construction site between towns of Luang Prabang and Vangvieng, local staffs outnumber Chinese workers. Nearby hilly villages have over 300 people while some 20 of them have been employed to work for Sinohydro 3. Lao staffs are learning the advanced technology and management from their Chinese colleagues.
>
> Chinese construction companies also donated money to local villages for building bridges and roads.

And not only roads, I saw and photographed new workshops, hotels, small factories and hospitals, along the road from Luang Prabang to Phonesai Village.

This is all part of Belt and Road Initiative, an optimistic, internationalist plan of China and its leadership, designed to connect lift out from poverty, a great number of nations, among them various previously colonized and plundered (by the West) countries in all corners of the globe.

***

While the Chinese workers are sweating, constructing the future of Laos, several French-speaking tourists on the main street of Luang Prabang are having beer.

In 1995, UNESCO inscribed this ancient capital of Laos onto the world heritage list. Mass tourism, mainly from the West, followed.

Restored strictly the 'French-way' into a sentimental, colonialist nostalgia 'living museum', Luang Prabang caters mainly to European tastes. The local people are here predominantly to serve, to 'just be there' for decorative purposes; poor and 'native', humble, selling craft, sitting on the asphalt and making sure to look appropriately destitute but 'friendly'.

There are a few posh boutiques and high-end hotels in town. No Laotian person could ever be able to afford a glass of Belgian beer on offer, or a meal in one of identical 'traditional' restaurants.

Signs are in English, sometimes in French and Laotian, but very rarely in Chinese.

Official Communist flags of Laos have almost entirely disappeared from the main streets of Luang Prabang.

In a local library, I am told by Mr. Seng Dao, who is the main librarian:

> Foreigners, mainly Europeans, used to come to local people and ask, sarcastically, even aggressively: "Why do you show Communist flags here? Or: "Why do you have Communist history in your books?"

Within few years, in the center of the city, the proud Communist legacy and identity of Laos has almost been entirely replaced with mass-produced low-quality silk, banal toys and other kitsch catering to the Western cultural fundamentalists, mainly from Europe.

But Laos is a Communist country, and flags are still waving in the wind as a rebellion, from various tuk-tuks and from the houses.

***

At UXO (Unexploded Ordinance) Center in Luang Prabang, I was unceremoniously kicked out, as they were expecting the visit of 'her royal highness', Princess Beatrice. A member of the vile British royal family responsible for the horrendous colonialist legacy all over the world (including Southeast Asia), Ms. Beatrice came to Luang Prabang mainly to attend a charity gala at the newly built Pullman hotel (where I happened to be staying). She addressed 230 guests, most of them Western 'expats' – predominantly men who have settled in and around Luang Prabang.

Rumors spoke of the possibility of collecting enough money to build a bigger structure for UXO office in the city.

I used to work in Laos, on several occasions, but especially in 2006, when I reported on the activities of the British de-mining agency MAG, in the devastated Plain of Jars.

For many years I have been passionate about this part of the world, trying to understand what really happened during the horrendous 'side-kick' wars initiated by the Empire: those in Cambodia and Laos.

In a beastly show of cruelty and indifference, the West

took millions of innocent human lives in Vietnam, Laos and Cambodia. We will never know the precise numbers, but combined, the death toll of the civilians most likely reached between 5 to 8 million. The West murdered and maimed people, and it poisoned entire huge areas of what was once known as 'Indochina'. And it got away with it, as it has done in virtually every corner of the world, where it brought genocide, thorough destruction and indescribable misery.

I spoke to dozens of local people in the Plain of Jars, using the services of my patient and deeply compassionate local interpreter, Mr. Luong.

There, in a small village of Ban Khai, Mr. Phommar who was then already 81 years old, revealed to me all the horrors of the so called "Secret War", unleashed by the West but particularly by the United States, against the scarcely populated Laos:

> We used to hide by the side of the road, in the ditch. Bombs kept falling and once our entire family was buried and we had to dig ourselves out. People were dying all around us. They used to bomb us with enormous airplanes which flew so high that we couldn't see or hear them approaching. And they used to send small planes which were looking for people on the ground; those flew so low that we were able to see faces in the cockpits.
>
> But the carpet bombing was the scariest. There was no warning. Bombs began to explode all around this area and we had no idea where they were coming from. On average, they bombed us five times a day. They bombed us almost every day, for more than ten years. Laos had only two million people then. And we were later told that the U.S. and its allies dropped three million tons of bombs on us.
>
> Eventually, nobody could survive here, anymore. Our houses were destroyed and our fields were full of unexploded substances. People were dying and so were the

animals. We had to leave and so we decided to go to Vietnam, to search for refuge. But the journey was tremendously arduous. We were moving at night, carrying few possessions. During the day we were hiding from the enemy planes.

The same was done, of course, to Cambodia, and to many parts of Vietnam.

Mr. Phommar concluded:

During the war I was very angry at Americans. I couldn't understand how can somebody be so brutal. How can somebody kill fellow human beings in such cold blood? But now my government tells me that everything is ok, that it is past and we should forget. But how can we forget? I don't feel angry anymore, but I would like the world to know what happened to us.

John Bacher, a historian and a Metro Toronto archivist once wrote about "The Secret War in Laos":

More bombs were dropped on Laos between 1965 and 1973 than the U.S. dropped on Japan and Germany during WWII. More than 350,000 people were killed. The war in Laos was a secret only from the American people and Congress.

Jeremy Kuzmarov described in detail and in full psychological horror, what the West did to Laotian men, women and children:

Military planners and "defense intellectuals" saw Laos as a testing ground for new forms of counterinsurgency and automated warfare the Pentagon had been developing, unencumbered by media or congressional scrutiny. A State Department official said: "This is [the] end of nowhere. We can do anything we want here because Washington doesn't seem to know that it exists. While USAID provided rice drops in the effort to win "hearts and minds," the military pioneered computer-directed bombing along with drone surveillance and dropped over 270 million cluster bombs, 80 million of which did not detonate... These strategies helped to delay the victory of the Pathet Lao revolutionary forces by over a decade, while providing a template for the automated warfare of the 21st century.

Conclusions of Jeremy Kuzmarov are chilling but precise:

If the Nazi activities represented a kind of apex to an age of inhumanity, American atrocities in Laos are clearly of a different order," Branfman wrote. "Not so much inhuman as a-human. The people of Na Nga and Nong Sa were not the object of anyone's passion. They simply weren't considered. What is most striking about American bombing in Laos is the lack of animosity felt by the killers to their victims. Most of the Americans involved have little if any knowledge of Laos or its people.

To put numbers into perspective, as reported by Santi Suthinithet, at Hyphen:

From 1964 to 1973, as part of the Secret War operation conducted during the Vietnam War, the US military dropped 260 million cluster bombs – about 2.5 million tons of munitions – on Laos over the course of 580,000 bombing missions. This is equivalent to a planeload of bombs being unloaded every eight minutes, 24 hours a day, for nine years – nearly seven bombs for every man, woman and child living in Laos.

In 2019, my credentials as a writer, film-maker and investigative journalist who was risking his life for Laos (and Cambodia), browsing through the minefields, interviewing victims of the beastly Western campaigns in this part of the world, got me, absolutely nowhere. Or more precisely, they got me just 5 minutes of a visit to the interior of UXO center. After that I got escorted to my car, so the safety of a member of mass-murderous British monarchy could be guaranteed.

Did Laos really need Princess Beatrice? It does not need charity, does it? The UK, together with the US, Australia, Thailand and few other nations were fully responsible for the death of at least 300,000 Laotian people. The West and its Asian allies killed here; they lied, and they have been covering it all up until today.

For experimenting on defenseless and innocent human beings, for ruining their land, poisoning rivers, slaughtering animals from the comfortable distance and height of the B-52 strategic bombers flight-paths, in an ideal, or even just 'normal' world, the West should be standing on its knees throwing ashes on its head, begging for forgiveness. Naturally, it should be paying war reparations amounting to trillions of dollars; to Laos, Vietnam and Cambodia. All this and much more it should be doing, to offset at least some of the monstrosities it committed, instead of throwing gala charity parties for the royal mafia, in the middle of 5-star establishments surrounded by local rice fields.

***

But we are not living in an ideal or even 'normal' world. The West is unapologetic. Despite everything, it feels morally superior to the rest of the world. It preaches its fundamentalist gospel. And here, in Laos, it is trashing China for pulling this wonderful gentle nation out of decades of horrors, misery and dependency.

Western propaganda against the Chinese projects in

Laos, is now in top gear.

Like in Africa, Western-financed NGO's are in full force in Vientiane and other cities of Laos. Instead of building or improving Laos, they are there just in order to push the Western agenda; to agitate against the Communist government and its projects and cooperation with China.

Bizarre and totally false stories are circulating in many major Western publications, accusing China of virtually everything, from not paying adequate wages, to ruining the Laotian environment.

The reason for all this propaganda war is clear: Laos is an extremely strategically-located country, bordering China, Burma, Cambodia, Thailand and Vietnam.

It is a Communist country. It is still very poor, but with tremendous potential. And now it is clearly aware of the fact that it can soon stand on its own feet.

China is capable and willing to transform this country, literally overnight, from a recipient of meager aid, to a powerful nation of 7 million inhabitants.

China is involved in building roads, railroads, hospitals, factories, workshops, as well as dams and hydroelectric power plants on the Mekong River. The latter is solving the notorious electricity shortages of Laos, while turning it into a net exporter of electricity, particularly to neighboring Thailand. It is also pulling hundreds of thousands of Laotian people out of poverty.

An article published on February 1, 2016 by NEO Magazine ("Laos: The new Cold War Battleground You Don't Know About") addresses the issue:

> Protesters paradoxically claim that the dams will disrupt both the environment and traditional fishing communities along rivers downstream from dams. Traditional fishing communities, however, are generally synonymous with both unsustainable environmental destruction and poverty.

Conversely, environmental impacts by dam construction can be mitigated through careful planning, while working to lift surrounding communities and the nation as a whole from poverty through improved infrastructure and cheaper and more accessible energy.

Protesters are not campaigning for careful planning, or better oversight of projects, they are campaigning instead for arrested development for Laos and its people – the sort of campaign only Wall Street and Washington could benefit from.

The West has built nothing substantial in Laos. And it is horrified by the possibility that under the Chinese leadership, Laos will provide an example to the world, proving that even a poor and once destroyed country could stand independent and tall, if it is helped by its mighty, ideologically close neighbor.

While the West is helping to build a few services in the old city, mainly for its own tourists and profits, China has already built the efficient Luang Prabang International airport, replacing the old tiny yellowish building that used to serve as a terminal.

Railroad and highway projects that will be passing through Laos will connect China with several countries of Southeast Asia, and secure for Laos substantial transit fees. It is a win-win situation, but not when observed from the point of view of those who just want the continuation of Western supremacy in the region and the rest of the world.

And what about the people of Laos? Is the West really treating them better than they are treated by the Chinese? This is what I learned from Mr. Seng, a Laotian supervisor working at a luxury international hotel 3 Nagas in Luang Prabang:

I am really glad that the Chinese are here. They are now

involved in many projects here in Laos, including power plants and this high-speed train project which will interlink Laos with China, Thailand and hopefully, Cambodia. Chinese are treating us very well. My brother works for them; he is a driver. He earns 900 dollars monthly. This is enormous amount of money here. In fact, Chinese are paying him 1.500 dollars, but the government here takes 600 as an income tax, or something... I work for a French hotel chain ACCOR, which is the biggest hotel company in the world, and I earn 200 dollars, as a supervisor. Local staff earns on average 120 dollars.

I checked with a French ACCOR employee who is based in Luang Prabang, and he confirmed the numbers.

The conclusions are clear: China pays local people the same wages as they pay to the Chinese workers. The French are paying local staff approximately 25-30 times less than what they pay their own people.

But search the internet: at least in the English language, and all you will find is an avalanche of fake news about the Chinese involvement in Laos. This is all that the world is allowed to know about this country, and its epic battle for true independence.

As always in the Western media: black is white, boys are girls, war is peace, and flamingos are pigs.

***

In the meantime, as I wrote earlier, the Communist flags have almost entirely disappeared from the center of Luang Prabang. It is because, I was told, the European tourists don't like to see them.

Yes, UNESCO supervised the preservation work of the old capital, but what is the result? Sentimental, feel-good 'colonial charm'; temples, silk shops and cafes with the

Western beer and free WIFI. Old Chinese-Lao architecture looks, suspiciously, French. Not a word about the horrors that the country had to go through in recent history; not a word that hundreds of people of Laos are still losing their lives due to the UXO, all over the country. Not a word about the French colonialism, the Western genocide during the so-called "Secret War", which was unleashed against the defenseless Laos.

And yes, not a word about the heroic Pathet Lao, and its superhuman struggle for a Communist fatherland, against the Western imperialist monsters.

On the outskirts of the city, predominantly European tourists visit the fake 'bear rescue center' (it is really nothing more than a depressing zoo for foreigners), overcrowded waterfalls and caves with religious motives. Hardly anyone goes to the real, tough and beautiful caves, where the Laotian patriots hid while they fought against the West.

Now the "National Museum" in the center of the city is basically an implanted (from abroad) glorification of the departed Laotian monarchy. While its shabby theatre shows, exclusively for foreign tourists and at an 'international price', several fragments of Ramayana. There are no visible monuments to the revolutionaries, and to the Communist heroes who forght for, and won contry's independence.

And the public library in the city center has, since several years ago, something called "The American Corner". You can find Allure there, Entrepreneur, Reader's Digest...

Mr. Seng Dao, my friend, a librarian, explains:

There is not much we can do. We can't just say 'no' to their corner, to their books. We cannot yet openly say 'no' to them, when it comes to so many things. But Lao people did not lose their memory. We know, we remember very well what was done to us. And our government reminds us; through our radio stations, through our press, our history books... in our own language.

In the old city, there are hardly any Chinese language signs. Yes, it is paradoxical, as the city is built in a Chinese style, although it now feels 'colonial', or call it Europeanized; catering to standardized, mainly ignorant German and French tastes.

As mentioned above, Lao people are supposed to look native, cute and poor. They do, here in the city. But only for now.

A few kilometers away from this pseudo-reality, from this over-sugary and to some extent treasonously demeaning tourist bordello, Chinese signs are proudly displayed, next or underneath Laotian writing. Chinese people, who are engaged in building Laos, prefer to live on the outskirts of Luang Prabang, together with local people, eating their food, sleeping in their guesthouses.

The presence of the Chinese engineers and workers is transforming, improving reality. Workshops are growing, eateries flourishing, and the real local economy is growing.

Further away from the city, powerful machines are roaring, drilling tunnels, building bridges. Laos is undergoing electrification; it is getting connected to the rest of the world through high-speed railroads and new highways. Schools and hospitals are being built, roads paved. Two Communist countries; two Asian sisters, side-by-side, are hard at work.

Nobody chases me away when I photograph Chinese construction sites. Proud smiles welcome me. Workers wave at me, or bow, and then, immediately, they go back to work. There is nothing to hide. There is no time to waste. This is reality; good, progressive reality!

Nothing is perfect, here or anywhere else in the world, but this is as good as it gets. I believe it is. I watch a giant construction site and people who are building the nation, raising it literally from the ashes, left by imperialism. The lenses of my glasses get foggy. Mekong is flowing below, and intact, pristine green mountains are resting in a tender embrace of white clouds.

I think: "The West dares to talk about 'environmental damage' here? Yet they have already ruined, thoroughly poisoned and literally liquidated some of the most pristine parts of the world that I know: Borneo, Papua, the Democratic Republic of Congo! How dare they?" But they do; they dare, and still getting away with it.

The nihilism, smear, filth that pours from the muzzles of the West and its regional servants, but it cannot deter this revolutionary optimism, which is so clearly detectable. It is simply beautiful to watch both Chinese and Laotian people working side by side, for a better world.

What did the countries that are attacking this tremendous effort, ever do for Laos? What has the West done for the people here? It colonized and enslaved Laos. And then, in one prolonged and truly incomprehensible horror show, carpet bombed, for years, the entire nation, murdering hundreds of thousands, without even declaring war against it!

How can the countries that committed genocide against Laos (and the entire world) be allowed to criticize Laos and China, belittling their efforts to improve lives of their people? And how come that Laotian people are still tolerating, even 'welcoming' Westerners in places like Luang Prabang, while they show clear disrespect for true essence of the Laotian state, for which so many local people sacrificed their lives? What are Westerners going to teach Laos, what can they teach, really: how to serve, how to be good obedient neo-colonial subjects?

Nobody needs that here, except the few members of the treasonous elites.

How can people like Princess Beatrice, or any of those 'royal' freaks be even allowed on the premises of such places as the UXO? The British royal family is the symbol of global colonialist holocaust. In their name, hundreds of millions of 'un-people' vanished, all over the world.

In the past, these were only rhetorical questions. Now such questions are being asked, in order to be answered.

What goes on in Laos is what I call the war between revolutionary optimism and Western nihilism (my latest book has the same title).

It is the last attempt of the monstrous Western imperialist culture to retain its control over the Planet.

Laos, in the past one of the most devastated countries on earth, is not going to allow being lectured to by its tormentor – the West – anymore. In the past, it fought, and against all odds it won. Now it is winning again. But the 'weapons' are different than in the days of the so-called "Secret War": they consist of high-speed railroad tracks, bridges and tunnels, mighty power-plants, hospitals and schools.

26 October 2018

West is Losing and so It's Bashing China and Russia 'Left and Right' Literally

*T*he insanity and vileness of Western anti-Chinese propaganda used to make some of my Chinese friends cry late at night. But things are changing. The lunacy of what is said and written about China (and Russia, of course), in the US and Europe, is now clearly reflecting frustration and the bad manners of sore losers. One could almost be inclined to pity the Western empire, if only it wasn't so violently murderous.

The Empire's propagandists are pitying nobody – they are now shooting like maniacs, but without any coherent plan.

Various Western 'experts' and journalists cannot really agree on the basics: 'what is really wrong with China'. But they are paid extremely well to find new and newer skeletons in the huge Chinese closets, and so they are constantly competing with each other, looking for the juiciest and the most scandalous stories. Often it appears that it pays to assume that absolutely everything is flawed with the most populous, and on top of it, Communist (with the 'Chinese characteristics, of course) country on earth!

China will end extreme poverty by 2020, but do not

look for cheers and applause from Berlin, Paris, London and Washington. China is far ahead of all the large countries on earth in building a so-called 'ecological civilization', but who is willing to notice? China is constructing public parks, boardwalks and playgrounds, the biggest on earth, but who cares? The Chinese government is introducing sweeping educational reforms, while flooding the entire nation with concert halls, museums and theatres. But that's not worth mentioning, obviously!

Western propaganda tries to discredit China literally from both 'left and right', sometimes accusing it for being too Communist, but when it is suitable, even for 'not being Communist enough'.

*The New York Tim*es ran a cover-page story on October 5, 2018, "Unlikely foe for China's leaders: Marxists". For this highly sarcastic piece, a reporter visited the Chinese city of Huizhou, from where he wrote about a group of over-zealous young Marxists who are demanding things to be as they were in Mao's days:

> But the Huizhou activists represent a threat the authorities did not expect.

Seriously? A threat? China is moving towards Communism, again, under the current leadership. We are talking about democratic, socially-oriented Communism. But let us not argue with the official U.S. newspaper. It is definitely not a pro-Communist publication, but they had to show some sympathy (by running a cover story!) to a small bunch of over-zealous 'opposition' Marxists, just to spread doubts among the readers, suggesting that the Chinese government is not that Red, anymore.

The next day (Saturday-Sunday edition, October 6-7, 2018), the same New York Times published two cover stories on China. One was along its usual anti-Chinese and anti-Russian conspiracy lines "Will China hack U.S. mid-terms?", but the other basically contradicted the story from the previous day, accusing Beijing this time of cutting the wings of private companies: "Beijing is pushing back into business", with a sub-title:

"Government flexes muscle as private companies that built economy lose ground."

'Wherever it can hurt China, just write it', could be the credo of thousands of European and North American journos: 'as long as the news about or from China is bad, really dark and negative, anything goes!'

Too much Communism, or too little... As far as the West is concerned – China can never get it right! Because... simply because it is China, because it is Asia, and because it waves the red flags.

And so, *The New York Times* ran two totally contradictory stories. An editorial blunder, or a pre-meditated attempt to inflict maximum damage, by kicking 'left and right'?

***

It is, of course, fun, to follow this propaganda trend, 'from a safe distance' (meaning: 'not believing a word of what it says'). But what is happening is not a joke; what is being done can actually be deadly. It can trigger, unexpectedly, a chain of events that could truly hurt China.

'An explosion' could originate in Taiwan, in Southeast Asia, or from the PRC territory itself.

Look at Brazil, look at Venezuela! Look at all those Color Revolutions, Umbrella Revolutions, 'Springs' from Europe to Arab countries. And look at China itself: who triggered; who sponsored the so-called Tiananmen

Square events? There is clearly enough evidence, by now, that it was not some spontaneous student rebellion.

The West has convinced several countries such as the Philippines, that they should confront China, through various territorial claims in which, honestly, almost no serious Filipino historian or political scientist is ready to believe (unless he or she got paid royally from abroad). I talked directly to several top historians and political scientists in Manila, and I got a clear picture of whom and what is behind those territorial claims. I wrote about it in the past, and soon will again.

China is too big to tolerate dangerous subversions from abroad. Its leadership knows well: when the country is in disarray, hundreds of millions of human beings suffer. To preserve the nation's territorial integrity is essential.

***

So, what is China really; in a summary?

It is a Communist (or you may call it a socialist) country with thousands of years of a great and comparatively egalitarian history. It has a mixed economy but with central planning (government tells the companies what to do, not vice-versa). It is clearly the most successful nation on earth when it comes to working on behalf of, and for the benefit of its citizens. It is also the most peaceful large nation on earth. And here are two more essential points: China is at the forefront of saving the world from the looming ecological disaster. And it has no colonies, or 'neo'-colonies, being essentially an 'internationalist' state.

Its political system, economy, culture: all are diametrically different from those in the West.

China has millions of things to say about how this planet should be governed, how it should be marching forward, and what is true democracy (rule of the people).

Now honestly: does Western mainstream, which manufactures 'public opinion' all over the world, allows many Chinese (PRC) patriots, Communists, thinkers, to appear on television screens, or to write op-eds?

We know the answer. Almost exclusively, it is the Westerners who are, (by the Western rulers), entrusted with the tremendous task of 'defining what China is or isn't'. And what the entire world is or isn't.

If China says that it is 'socialist with Chinese characteristics', they say 'No!' with their perfect Oxford accents. And their arrogance from telling the greatest civilization on earth what it actually is or isn't, gets accepted because of the fact that most of them are white, and they speak perfect English (paradoxically, still a seal of trustworthiness, at least in certain circles).

The West never hears what the Chinese or Russians think about the world. While the Chinese and Russians are literally bombarded by what the West thinks about them.

Even Chinese people used to listen to such 'false prophets' from the 'civilized West'. Now they know better. Same as the Russians know better. Same as many in Latin America know better.

The spread of Western propaganda and dogmas used to appear as a battle, an ideological combat, for Chinese and Russian brains (if not for hearts). Or at least it appeared as such, to many naïve, trusting people.

Now it is all much simpler and 'in the open': the battle continues, but the frontlines and goals have shifted. How?

What is taking place these days, is simply an enormous clash between Western imperialism plus its propaganda, versus the determination of the Chinese and Russian people to live their own lives the way they choose. Or to put it into even simpler terms: the battle is raging between Western imperialism on one side, and democracy with 'Chinese and Russian characteristics' on the other.

West is bashing China and Russia 'left and right', literally. But it is definitely not winning!

14 October 2018

Despite Western skepticism, democracy thrives in China

Almost every year, just before the annual sessions of the National People's Congress, the country's top legislature, and the Chinese People's Political Consultative Conference National Committee, the country's top political advisory body, some people have claimed the two great institutions play the role of rubber stamps, and China's democracy cannot truly represent the people.

Criticism of the Chinese system comes mostly from abroad. But even some Chinese critics have been, from time to time, influenced by these foreign perceptions.

China is often analyzed and judged strictly according to Western norms and rules, which is chauvinistic and amazingly patronizing, to say the least. However, China, with thousands of years of history and culture, deserves to be defined and judged by its own people and according to its own measures.

The term democracy is derived from the Greek language. It loosely means "rule of the people". But it doesn't stipulate that a truly democratic country has to follow a Western multi-party/corporate model, or more concretely, a model in which big corporations and "powerful individuals" finance political campaigns (while backing particular candidates), and to all intents and purposes select the government.

There should be different models of democracy - different models of "rule of the people". And good democracy means the government should serve the people.

In the West, and in its "client states", most of the ordinary people are destined to serve the interests of corporations, with the government making sure they do not break "the rules". For instance, the United States is often cited as the "perfect model" of Western democracy. But under the US style of democracy, vested interest groups often play a bigger role in people's lives. For instance, shootings in schools have wreaked havoc in US society and ordinary US citizens have been strongly advocating gun control. But such contentions always fall on deaf ears, because the powerful gun lobby can block gun-control bills in the Congress.

China simply cannot and should not follow such a model of democracy. Chinese citizens have fought hard for their independence, and they have struggled during the great revolutionary war, in order to create a system that has been serving the people. After great sacrifices, the people of China have achieved their goal. The system is theirs, as it works to improve their lives and livelihoods. It is evolving into a system that is truly "of the people" and "for the people".

And Chinese leaders are listening attentively to their people.

When the Chinese nation needed a stronger economy and better livelihoods, the Communist Party of China headed by late leader Deng Xiaoping launched sweeping reforms four decades ago. And when problems such as growing inequality, environmental degradation and other negative by-products of rapid economic growth emerged, the Party addressed people's call again. The CPC with Xi Jinping as its core has put great emphasis on the environment ("ecological civilization"), on the great Chinese culture, and above all on improving the lives of all Chinese people by eradicating extreme poverty. The powerful and progressive model of "Socialism with Chinese characteristics" has stepped into a new era.

China has developed a different development path from that of the West, but it still has made great contributions to world peace and prosperity through programs such as the **Belt and Road Initiative** and a "shared future for humankind", which shows China's democracy is not only serving the Chinese people but also the peoples of the rest of the world by facilitating regional and global development for the improvement of human lives, while at the same time respecting local cultures and differences.

28 February 2018

China's success here to stay

*D*espite being repeatedly proved wrong, proponents of the "China collapse" theory have been using it to win their "share of the propaganda market". A recent article by Gordon G. Chang in Foreign Policy, a bimonthly US magazine, is one such example.

Even though there is nothing truly "revolutionary" in Chang's arguments and predictions, some Western politicians, media outlets and scholars are attaching extraordinary importance to him. In his book, The Coming Collapse of China, Chang predicted that China would "collapse" in 2006. When he saw China was not only still there, but also developing at an accelerated rate, he modified his "prophecy" slightly, giving the country a few more years to live - until 2011.

This is 2012, and I have just left China (Beijing, to be precise) after spending a wonderful few days there. The country looked far from collapsing. In fact, it is well-positioned; thousands of miles away from most Western capitals with their angry, dissatisfied crowds frustrated by social malaise. Obviously realizing that China has once again defied his nihilist predictions, Chang apologized to his readers and deferred the doomsday scenario to 2012.

Here are some arguments to show how unoriginal

Chang's offerings are, at least from the point of view of the Western conservative mainstream:

> The global boom of the last two decades ended in 2008, China, which during its reform era had one of the best demographic profiles of any nation, will soon have one of the worst. The Chinese workforce will level off in about 2013, perhaps 2014 a trend that will eventually make the country's factories uncompetitive.

Above all, Chang argues:

> China's 'sweet spot' is over because, in recent years, the conditions that created it have either disappeared or will soon.

What is fascinating is that Chang is actually redefining what is conservative and what is progressive to suit his political and ideological goals. He calls pro-business reforms "progressive" and sees the recent reforms in China, which are expected to benefit people, as most negative.

What Chang and his ilk find most threatening is the looming re-establishment of "barriers to international commerce". To make it clear, the welfare of Chinese people does not matter one bit to them. What is important for them is the access of Western companies to the Chinese markets. Eminent American linguist, cognitive scientist and activist Noam Chomsky calls it "profit over people".

Chang is forgetting that we are living in the 21st century, which is marked by the "rebellion" of countries previously bullied by the West. These countries are now successfully pursuing their own political and economic models - Venezuela, Bolivia, Argentina, Ecuador and others. In Europe and the United States, the majority of the people are disgusted with pro-market fundamentalism that has kidnapped their nations, but they cannot do much to change the system. They are searching for alternatives, looking at Latin America and China, but also at homegrown options.

If anything is collapsing, it is the group of nations governed by market fundamentalism.

China, Russia and Latin America are, thank you, just fine: both economically and psychologically. They are growing at astonishing rates in an era of sluggish global growth not to satisfy some business entities but to improve the lives of their people. For them, economy and trade are the means, not the end.

This spirit of unity, solidarity and enthusiasm is exactly what makes China successful and unstoppable. It is also what makes its enemies desperate and confrontational in anticipation of defeat.

There is no doubt that Chinese people, the Communist Party of China and the Chinese government will thrive in and after 2012. But China and its people should be aware of and vigilant against the dangers they face from outside: reports like those prepared by right-wingers are not just miscalculated predictions. They are well-planned targeted attacks against the Chinese system, an attempt to frustrate and destabilize the country, to confuse its people, to break their zeal of building a prosperous, compassionate and egalitarian society.

It goes without saying that the majority of Chinese people want social justice. They want to build a decent and prosperous country, for themselves and for their children. Reforms in China are a logical response of the government to the desires of the people. Such a process is called democracy, which actually translates into "the rule of the people", not "the Western-style political system".

As long as China is united in building a better and just society, it will be around not only at the end of this year, but also for centuries and millenniums to come. In the future, Chang and his followers and other proponents of China's collapse will make and modify their well-financed but futile predictions.

30 January 2012

Note: Editing this essay/chapter at the end of 2019, I have to testify that China is still alive and well.

Now it is fighting not only for its own future (no poverty after 2020, Ecological Civilization, etc.), but also for the internationalist dream of "BRI" (Belt and Road Initiative).

Progress that China made since 2012, when the essay first .went to print, is enormous. Regression registered by the Western nations in the same period of time, is enormous as well.

Road of love on the path to development

Eight years after its inauguration, "China Road" is still the best road in Kenya. After driving over countless bumps, and around potholes, roadblocks around Nairobi, it is a balm to the nerves and salvation to suspensions and tires. The 150-km-long stretch of black asphalt is smooth, its shoulders are wide and lanes divisions well marked. I hardly notice my Land Rover has reached a speed of 140 km an hour.

"Chinese engineers working here were eating snails," laughs Musa Mwandima, a Kenyan employed during the construction of the road that was inaugurated in August 2001. "And one foreman who always talked to me explained that here in Africa we have too many children. He explained to me the one-child policy in China. He said we should not have many children in such a poor country. Otherwise, how could they be fed and educated? At that time I had two kids. I wanted to have eight, but I decided to strike a compromise - after the Chinese left, I settled for only three."

Mwandima's smile is warm. He pauses, lost in memories, remembering much better days when his dusty humble village - Kasarani Voi - came suddenly to life. Heavy equipment were raising dust, powerful lights were penetrating the night, and he felt like being part of a team building a better future for his country.

Since then economic crises, drought and tribal violence have devastated Kenya again, but the China Road still cuts through stunning countryside: It's a monument to engineering excellence and goodwill, and a glimmer of hope for the local people.

"There was a language barrier and we couldn't communicate much with the Chinese people," says Mwandima, "but they respected us - there was no racism whatsoever. We were paid more than by local companies and we were always paid on time and with all the extras, such as overtime, that were due."

China Road, also known as the trans-Africa highway, is an important stretch of thoroughfare connecting the coast with Nairobi. This is easily the most important artery in East Africa. Heavy trucks move goods from Mombasa, Kenya's largest port, to the rest of the country and further to Uganda, Rwanda, and Burundi and even to Goma in the eastern part of the Democratic Republic of Congo. As the railroad system continues to deteriorate, Kenya is now more dependent on its road network for transporting goods and people.

China Road begins at Mtito Andei town near the gate to Ngai National Park. In the other direction, between Mtitio Andei and Nairobi, the road is called the "German Road" because it was built by a German construction company with European Union funds.

From Mtito Andei, China Road cuts through some stunning landscape, including the enormous Tsavo National Park with the Ngulia Rhino Sanctuary and several luxury safari lodges and camps a short driving distance away.

My "guide" to the area, Mghanga Mwandawiro, one of the main leaders of Kenyan opposition and chairman of the Social Democratic Party, explains: "China Road connects the coastal province with the eastern province. This is an extremely good, viable and necessary development project. It has not only improved the main transportation route, but also brought my own village, Werugha, closer to Mombasa and the rest of the country. It has connected hundreds of other villages as well. We are very grateful to the Chinese government. We are also thankful to China for building the first university in Taita district at Mariwenyi."

The Jomo Kenyatta University of Agriculture and Technology with its Taita-Taveta Campus can be seen from the road and the Kasarani Voi village. It blends beautifully with the dramatic landscape, with the Vuria Mountain as its backdrop.

Workers who have gathered on the roadside to talk with Mwandawiro and me do not seem in any hurry to leave. They keep exchanging old stories about their participation in the enormous engineering project that changed their lives.

"What impressed us the most was how hard the Chinese worked", says Mghenyi-Keke. "We worked next to them, but we were also observing them, trying to learn how they kept up such a high working morale. And they were absolutely punctual. When they said 9 o'clock, that's what it had to be. Their equipment were always functioning, and their construction materials always ready."

"I would like to go to China one day," says Mwandima. "People I worked with were very kind and patient with us. When we committed a mistake, they didn't scream at or insult us. They just explained how to improve things

Working with the Chinese made me realize that we know so little, almost nothing about their country. And it is one of the biggest countries in the world, isn't it? We know that they produce many things, even the spare parts for our bicycles. But we know almost nothing about how they live. We always try to watch films about China on TV now, but the offering is very limited."

After sunset, Mwandawiro and I drive up and down the Chinese Road, stopping for dinner and a cup of coffee, talking to people. One of the leading Marxists in Africa, Mwandawiro knows personally many world leaders, including Fidel Castro, Bolivian President Evo Moralez, Venezuelan President Hugo Chavez. But he has never visited an Asian country and now wants to know more about China.

I share what I know of China from my visits to Beijing, Shanghai and other Chinese cities. "China should really do more to promote itself, especially its culture," Mwandawiro says.

Late at night he asks me to turn left; to leave the main road and kill the engine.

Our headlights now illuminate a prison gate. Guards rush out, but after recognizing him as "their MP" they salute and leave us to park in front of the gate.

"This is the historic prison of Manyani, the place where during the struggle for independence, British colonial rulers tortured our freedom fighters," Mwandawiro says. "The torture they inflicted here was extreme and brutal. It was one of the first concentration camps on earth. And nobody could escape because the nearest town was 70 km away and all this area was and still is inhabited by wild animals. You wouldn't stay alive for more then a few minutes if you tried to run away.

"I brought you here to make a point: Some countries

came to Africa to build prisons and camps, others came to build roads."

22 July 2009

Note: China continues to build roads and railroads all over East Africa. Now, "Chinese Railroad" is connecting coastal city of Mombasa with the capital, Nairobi. Soon, entire East Africa will be linked by modern rail network.

Hong Kong
Appendix

Western media portrays Hong Kong hooligans as heroes. But are they?

$\mathcal{W}$henever Hong Kong protesters are destroying public property, there are no cameras of Western media outlets in sight. But when police decide to intervene, protecting their city, Western media crusaders emerge in full force.

On Sunday, huge US flags were waving in the air. A massive demonstration, consisting of mainly young people, was moving up from the old British-built downtown area of the city towards the US Consulate General, often erroneously called the "*embassy*."

The temperature was well over 30 degrees Celsius, but the number of 'protesters' kept growing. Many of the main arteries in Hong Kong were entirely blocked.

Western media were there in full force, wearing yellow fluorescent vests, their 'Press' insignia, helmets and masks. They mingled with the crowd, filming US flags, clearly enjoying the show.

"*President Trump, Please Liberate Hong Kong,*" I read on several posters.

"*Liberate from whom?*" I asked a cluster of protesters, all of them in ninja outfits, metal bars in their hands, black scarves covering their faces.

Several of them replied, mumbling something incomprehensible. One girl shouted defiantly:

"*From Beijing!*"

"*But Hong Kong is China, isn't it?*" I asked. "*How could it be liberated from itself?*"

"*No! Hong Kong is Hong Kong!*" came a ready-made reply.

Nearby, I spotted British Union Jack, with old colonial-era Hong Kong coat of arms.

The big demonstration was clearly treasonous. Its members delivered a petition to the US consulate general, demanding that the US Congress pass legislation that would require its government to monitor and decide whether Hong Kong is 'autonomous enough' from the PRC, and whether it should then qualify for US trade and economic benefits.

All over the downtown area, hundreds of 'ninjas' were shouting pro-Western slogans. Here British-era HK flags were being waved, alongside the US flags.

I approached a young couple among the protesters, who were resting on a bench:

Do your friends realize how brutal, undemocratic and oppressive was British rule? Do they know in what misery many Hong Kong citizens had to live in that era? And about censorship, humiliation…?

"*No!*" They shouted at me, outraged. "*It is all propaganda!*"

"*Whose propaganda?*" I wondered.

"*The propaganda of Beijing. Communist propaganda!*"

At least they spoke some English. A bizarre thing about Hong Kong is that, while some people here would like to (or are perhaps paid to say that they'd want to?) have the

British colonial administration back, a great majority of the people hardly speak any English now, while also refusing to speak Mandarin. Little wonder that Hong Kong is quickly losing its edge to the pro-Chinese and highly cosmopolitan Singapore!

But the demonstration was not where 'the action' really was and I knew it, intuitively.

The flag-waving march was a big staged event for the Western mass media. There, 'pro-democracy' slogans were chanted in an orderly manner. Nothing was burned, vandalized or dismantled wherever European or North American press cameras were present!

A few blocks away, however, I witnessed monstrous vandalizing, of one of the entrances to the Central subway (MTR) station. Hooligans who call themselves 'protesters' were ruining public property, a transportation system used by millions of citizens every day.

While they were at it, they also dismantled public metal railings that separate sidewalks from roadways. Metal bars from this railing were later utilized for further attacks against the city infrastructure, as well as against the police.

Umbrellas in the hands of 'protesters' were covering the crime scene. Umbrellas similar to those used in 2014, during the previous, so-called 'Umbrella Uprising.'

No foreign reporters were in sight! This was not for the world. This was raw, real, and brutal.

"*Don't film!*" covered mouths began shouting at me.

I kept filming and photographing. I was not wearing any press jacket or helmet or Press insignia. I never do, anywhere in the world.

They left me alone; too busy destroying the street. As they were dismantling public property, their backpacks, stuffed with portable players, were regurgitating the US national anthem.

My friend from Beijing wrote me a brief message:

> They are selling their own nation and people. We have very bad words for them in Chinese.

But it is not only mainland China that is disgusted with what is happening in Hong Kong. Three major Hong Kong-based newspapers, Wen Wei Po, Ta Kung Pao and Hong Kong Commercial Daily, are all pro-Beijing, pro-police and are defining 'protesters' as "*rioters*" or "*troublemakers*" (in Chinese).

Among the big ones, only Ming Pao and Apple Daily, which are traditionally anti-Beijing, are defining 'protesters' as 'gatherers', 'protesters' and even "liberators."

Local citizens are mainly (as they'd been during the 2014 riots) hostile to the 'protests' but are scared to confront the mainly young, covered and armed (with metal bars and clubs) gangs. Some tried to, even in a luxury mall in the center of the city, and were brutally beaten.

'Protesters' seem to be on adrenalin, and in a highly militant mood. They gather and move in hordes. Most of them refuse to speak.

What is important to understand is that, while the rioters are trying to spread the message that they are 'fighting for democracy,' they are actually highly intolerant to all those who disagree with their goals. In fact, they are violently attacking those with different opinions.

Furthermore, and this I have to spell out, after covering protests in literally hundreds of cities worldwide, from Beirut to Lima, Buenos Aires, Istanbul, Paris, Cairo, Bangkok and Jakarta: what is happening in Hong Kong is extremely mild when it comes to police responses! Hong Kong police run well and fast. It created human chains, flashed a lot of light and sporadically used tear gas. It defends itself when attacked. But violence?

If you compare police actions here to those in Paris, it is all politeness and softness. Hardly any rubber bullets. Tear gas is 'honest' and not mixed with deadly chemicals, like it is in many other places, and administered in small doses. No water cannon spitting liquid full of urine and excrement, as in many other cities of the world. Trust me: I am an expert in tear gas. In Istanbul, during the Gezi Park uprising, protesters had to use gas masks, so did I. Otherwise you'd faint or end up in a hospital. People are also fainting in Paris. No one is fainting here; this is mild stuff.

As for the 'other side,' the level of violence from the protesters is extreme. They are paralyzing the city, ruining millions of lives. The number of foreign arrivals in Hong Kong is down 40 percent. Reception at the Mandarin Oriental Hotel, which is right next to Sunday's battles, told me that most of the rooms are now empty, and during the 'events', the hotel is cut off from the world.

And what about their traitorous demands? Would this be accepted anywhere in the world? Flying flags of a foreign country (in this case, of the USA) and demanding intervention?

Hong Kong *"pro-democracy activist leaders"* like Joshua Wong are clearly colluding with Western interests and governments. He and others are spreading, constantly, what anywhere else would be described as fake news. For instance, *"My town is the new Cold War's Berlin,"* he recently declared. Yes, perhaps, but not because of the HK government, but because of his own actions and the actions of people like himself.

Coverage of events by Western mass media is clearly selective and that is putting it mildly. Actually, many media outlets from Europe and North America are 'adding fuel to the fire.' They are encouraging rioters while exaggerating the actions of local police. I am monitoring and filming their work and what I see is outrageous!

I am writing this report in Tai Kwun Center. Now world-famous art complex (of the "*new, Chinese Hong Kong*"), this used to be the Central Police Station under the British occupation, as well as so-called Victoria Prison Compound.

Mr. Edmond, who works for the center, explains:

> If there was a referendum now, the so-called protesters would not win. They would lose. This is an internal issue of China, and it should be treated as such. A continuation of the 2014 events. What changed this time is that the protesters are opting for extreme violence now. People of Hong Kong are scared; scared of them, not of the authorities.

Here, prisoners were confined and executed, during British rule. Not far away from here, monstrous slums were housing deprived subjects of the queen. After the Brits left, those slums were converted to public parks.

Life in Hong Kong improved. Not as fast as in neighboring Shenzhen or Guangzhou, but it improved. The reason Hong Kong is being 'left behind' is because of its antiquated British-era laws, rules and regulations, its extreme capitalist system; because of "*too little of Beijing*", not "*because of too much of it.*"

These hooligans are going against the interests of their own people, and their own people are now cursing them. Not loudly, yet, as rioters have clubs and metal bars, but cursing.

Western media chooses not to hear these curses. But China knows. It hears. I hear Hong Kong people, too.

Chinese curses are terrifying, powerful. And they do

not dissolve in thin air.

10 September 2019

Andre Vltchek

Some in Hong Kong Feel Frustrated, as Their City is Losing to Mainland China

$\mathcal{H}$ong Kong is losing to Mainland China. Its poverty rates are high, it suffers from corruption and savage capitalism. It is now the most expensive city on earth. People are frustrated, but paradoxically, they are blaming socialist Beijing for their problems, instead of the legacy of British colonialism. 'Across the line', Shenzhen, Shanghai, Beijing, Xiang and other cities are leaving Hong Kong behind in almost all fields.

When my dear friend and a great concert pianist from Beijing, Yuan Sheng, used to live in New York, recording, giving concert and teaching at prestigious Manhattan School of Music, he told me that he used to cry at night: "In the United States, they smear China. I felt hurt, defenseless".

He returned to Beijing, gave back his Green Card and began teaching at Beijing Conservatory. He never regretted his decision. "Beijing is much more exciting than New York, these days", he told me.

It is obvious that Beijing is booming: intellectually,

artistically; in fact, in all fields of life.

Yuan's friend, who returned from London and became a curator at the iconic "Big Egg" (the biggest opera house on earth), shared her thoughts with me:

> I used to sit in London, frustrated, dreaming about all those great musicians, all over the world. Now, they come to me. All of them want to perform in Beijing. This city can make you or break you. Without being hyperbolic, this is now one of the most important places on earth. Just under one roof, in one single night, we can have a Russian opera company performing in our big halls, in another one there is a Chinese opera, and a Bolivian folklore ensemble in a recital hall. And this is only one of Beijing's theatres.

When the Chinese artists and thinkers are fighting for the prime with their Western counterparts, it is usually Beijing, Shanghai and Shenzhen, 'against' London, Paris and New York. Hong Kong is 'somewhere there', behind, suddenly a backwater.

While Hong Kong University and the City University of Hong Kong used to be the best in China, many Mainland institutions of higher learning, including Peking University and Tsinghua, are now producing many more cutting-edge creative thinkers. I spoke at all of these schools, and can confirm that the young people in Beijing and Shanghai are extremely hardworking, endlessly curious, while in Hong Kong, there is always that mildly arrogant air of exceptionalism, and lack of discipline.

It used to be that the so-called "Sea Turtles" (students who went abroad and to Hong Kong, and then returned to Mainland China), were treated like celebrities, but now, it is much easier to get a job with the Mainland China's diplomas.

Recently, while filming the riots in Hong Kong, I was

told by a receptionist at one of the major shopping plazas:

> We do not treat visitors from Mainland China well. And, they lost interest in Hong Kong. Before, they used to come here, to admire out wealth. Now, most of them are avoiding this place. What we have, they have, too, and often better. If they travel, they rather go to Bangkok or Paris.

These days, the contrast between Xiang, Shanghai, Beijing and Hong Kong is shocking. Mainland infrastructure is incomparably better. Public areas are vast, and cultural life much more advanced than that in a former British colony.

While the Mainland Chinese cities have almost no extreme poverty, (and by the end of 2020 will have zero), in Hong Kong, at least 20% are poor, and many simply cannot afford to live in their own city. Hong Kong is the most expensive place on earth. Just to park a car in could easily cost over US$700 per month, for just working hours. Tiny apartments cost over a million US dollars. Salaries in Hong Kong, however, are not higher than those in London, Paris or Tokyo.

The city is run by an extreme capitalist system, 'planned' by corrupt tycoons/developers. The obsolete British legal system here is clearly geared to protect the rich, not the majority. That was essentially why the "Extradition Bill" was proposed: to protect Hong Kong inhabitants from the unbridled, untouchable, as well as unelected de facto rulers.

But there is this 'deal', negotiated before Hong Kong was returned where it belongs, which is – to China. "One country, two systems". It is an excellent contract for the turbo-capitalist magnates, and for the pro-Western "activists". And it is extremely bad one for the average people of Hong Kong. Therefore, after months of riots sponsored by the West, the Hong Kong administration scrambled the bill.

***

Young hooligans know very little about their city. I talked to them, extensively, during their first anti-Beijing riots in 2014 (so-called "Umbrella Revolution").

Correctly, then and now they have been frustrated about the declining standards of living, about the difficulties to get well-paid jobs and find affordable housing. They told me that 'there is no future for them', and that 'their lives are going nowhere'.

But quickly, their logic would collapse. While realizing what tremendous progress, optimism and zeal could be observed in the People's Republic of China, under the leadership of the Communist Party, they would still be demanding more capitalism, which is actually ruining their territory. In 2014, and now, they are readily smearing the Communist Party.

Being raised on the shallow values of selfishness and egotism, they are now betrayed their own country, and began treasonous campaigns, urging foreign powers, including US and UK, to "liberate them". All for just fleeting moment of fame, for a "selfie uprising".

To liberate from whom? China does not, (unfortunately for Hong Kong), interfere in Hong Kong's economic and social affairs. If anything, it builds new infrastructure, like an enormous bridge now connecting Hong Kong with Macau (a former Portuguese colony) and a high-speed train system, linking Hong Kong with several cities in Mainland China.

More restrain Beijing shows, more it gets condemned by the rioters and Western media, for 'brutality'. More subway stations and public property get destroyed by rioters, more sympatry flows for them from the German, US and British right-wing politicians.

***

For decades, the British colonialists were humiliating people of Hong Kong, while simultaneously turning their city into a brutal, and by the Asian standards, ruthless and fully business oriented megapolis. Now people are confused and frustrated. Many are asking, who they really are?

For Hong Kong, this is a difficult moment of soul-searching.

Even those who want to "go back to UK", can hardly speak English. When asked "why do they riot", they mumble something about 'democracy' and 'freedom' in the West, plus 'evilness of Beijing'. Brochures of some obscure, extremist Japanese religious cults get distributed. It is one big intellectual chaos. Rioters know nothing about Syria, Afghanistan, Venezuela, countries which are being ruined by the West.

Leaders like Joshua Wong are proudly colluding with the Western embassies. To praise Chinese socialism publicly is now dangerous – people get beaten by the "pro-democracy" rioters, for such "crimes".

Highly educated and overly-polite Singapore is literally sucking out hundreds of foreign companies from Hong Kong. Its people speak both English and Mandarin. In Hong Kong, great majority speaks only Cantonese. Many foreigners are also relocating to Shanghai. Not only big businesses: Shanghai is now full of European waiters.

Even tourism is down in Hong Kong, by 40%, according to the recent data.

Absurdly: the rioters want precisely what the Communist Party of China is providing: they want real struggle against corruption, as well as determined attempt to solve housing crises, create new jobs, and provide more public services. They want better education, and generally better life. They want "Shanghai or Beijing", but they say that they want to be a colony of the UK, or a dependency of the USA.

They loosely define communist goals, and then they shout that they are against Communism.

***

China is now ready to celebrate its 70th Anniversary of the Founding of The People's Republic of China.

Clearly, the West is using Hong Kong to spoil this great moment.

After leaving Hong Kong, in Shanghai, I visited a brilliant, socialist realism exhibition at the iconic, monumental China Art Museum. Country under the leadership of President Xi is once again confident, revolutionary and increasingly socialist; to horror of declining West. It is a proud nation with great, elegant cities constructed by the people, for the people, and with progressively ecological countryside. Its scientific, intellectual and social achievements speak louder than words.

Contrast between Hong Kong and Shanghai is tremendous, and growing.

But do not get me wrong: I like Hong Kong. I have more than 20 years of history with that old, neurotic and spoiled lady. I can feel her pulse. I love old trams and ferries, and out-of-the-way islands.

But Hong Kong's charm lies in its decay.

Mainland China's beauty is fresh. China is one of the oldest cultures on earth, one of the deepest. But it feels crisp, full of hope and positive energy. Together with its closest ally, Russia, it is now working and fighting for the entire world; it is not selfish.

Hong Kong is fighting only for its vaguely defined uniqueness. Actually, it is not Hong Kong that is fighting, as most of people there want to be where they truly belong – in their beloved nation – China. It is a gang of kids with their face-masks that is fighting. In brief: a relatively big group of pro-Western extremists, whose leaders are putting their fame above the interests of the people.

***

Hong Kong has no "Big Egg"; no famous theatre where the greatest musicians are stunning the world. Its only art museum is closed for reconstruction, for years, and will re-open only at the end of 2019. Its cultural life is shallow, even laughable, for the place which is branding itself as the "Asia's World City". There are no great discoveries made here. It is all business. Big, big business. And creeping decay.

Beijing could 'liberate' Hong Kong, easily; to give it purpose, pride and future.

But young hooligans want to be liberated by Washington, instead. They want to be re-colonized by London. And they do not consult their fellow citizens. That clearly reflects their idea about 'democracy'. Not the "rule of the people", but the "rule of the West".

Not only they feel spite for their country, but they also scorn and intimidate their fellow citizens who just want to have their meaningful life, based on the Chinese values.

3 October 2019

About Author

Philosopher, novelist, filmmaker, investigative journalist, poet, playwright, and photographer, Andre Vltchek is a revolutionary, internationalist and globetrotter.

In all his work, he confronts Western imperialism and the Western regime imposed on the world.

He has covered dozens of war zones and conflicts from Bosnia and Peru to Sri Lanka, DR Congo and Timor Leste.

His latest books are "China and Ecological Civilization" with John B. Cobb, Jr., "Revolutionary Optimism, Western Nihilism", "The Great October Socialist Revolution: Impact on the World and the Birth of Internationalism", "Exposing Lies of the Empire", "Fighting Against Western Imperialism" and "On Western Terrorism" with Noam Chomsky.

"Aurora" and "Point of No Return" are his major works of fiction written in English. "Nalezeny" is his novel written in Czech. His plays are "Ghost of Valparaiso" and "Conversations with James".

Other works include books of political non-fiction "Western Terror: From Potosi to Baghdad", "Indonesia: Archipelago of Fear", "Exile" (with Pramoedya Ananta Toer and Rossie Indira) and "Oceania".

He is a member of Advisory Committee of the BRussells Tribunal.

The investigative work of Andre Vltchek appears in countless publications worldwide. Andre Vltchek has produced and directed several documentary films for the left-wing South American television network teleSUR. They deal with diverse topics, from Turkey/Syria to Okinawa, Kenya, Egypt and Indonesia, but all expose the effects of Western imperialism on the Planet.

His feature documentary film "Rwandan Gambit" has been broadcasted by PressTV, and aims at reversing the official narrative on the 1994 genocide, as well as exposing the Rwandan and Ugandan plunder of DR Congo on behalf of Western imperialism.

He produced a feature length documentary film about the Indonesian massacres of 1965 in "Terlena - Breaking of a Nation", as well as his film about the brutal Somali refugee camp, Dadaab, in Kenya: "One Flew Over Dadaab". Hid documentary film "On Western Terrorism" is his lengthy debate with Noam Chomsky on the state of the world.

He frequently speaks at revolutionary meetings, as well as at the principal universities worldwide.

He presently lives in Asia and the Middle East.

His website is: http://andrevltchek.weebly.com/

And his twitter is: @AndreVltchek

Andre Vltchek